WELCOME TO JAPAN

LAND OF SAKURA, SAKE, SUSHI AND SHINTO

Sathyamurthy Vaman

Clever Fox® PUBLISHING
Chennai • Bangalore

CLEVER FOX PUBLISHING
Chennai, India

Published by CLEVER FOX PUBLISHING 2025

ISBN: 978-93-6707-578-4

CONTENTS

QUICK GLANCE AT THE LAND OF THE RAISING SUN

Japan is an "archipelago" with four main islands: Honshu, Hokkaido, Shikoku, and Kyushu. These four islands, along with numerous smaller islands, make up the Japanese territory. Additionally, Okinawa, part of the Ryukyu archipelago, is also considered a significant island.

Japan is traditionally divided into eight main regions. These regions, while not formal administrative units, are commonly used for geographical and cultural categorization. The eight regions are Hokkaido, Tohoku, Kanto, Chubu, Kinki (or Kansai), Chugoku, Shikoku, and Kyushu.

In the context of Japan, there are 47 prefectures (known as *todōfuken*), which rank immediately below the national government. They form the country's first level of jurisdiction and administrative division. Each Japanese prefecture has its own unique characteristics, but the general principles of funding and management apply.

Regions

Hokkaido

The main advantage of this region is its natural environment, allowing the area to have the highest levels of production in agriculture and fisheries.

Tohoku

Tohoku region is specialized in the electrical machinery and food industry sectors. Among Tohoku's trading partners, Asia and North America are in top positions.

Kanto

Kanto region functions as Japan's greatest launch-pad for new businesses and industries, and with Tokyo located in it, the region can be considered Japan's engine.

Chubu

Chubu region accounts for 20% of the nationwide share in shipments of manufactured goods and is a catalyst driving the Japanese economy with its manufacturing base.

Kansai

The Kansai region in Japan is located in the heart of Japan. Including the three major cities of Kyoto, Osaka and Kobe, the Kansai region has the nation's second-largest economy, with a population of over 20 million.

Chugoku

The Chugoku Region includes research and development businesses in the fields of electronics, biotechnology, and new materials, and is leading the world with its advanced technical power.

Shikoku

Agriculture industries are well developed in the region and provide a gross domestic product that is higher than the average when compared to other areas of Japan.

Kyushu & Okinawa

Thanks to their location, both Kyushu and Okinawa are strategic regions for Japan to connect with nearby Korea, China, and the whole East Asia region in general.

Each prefecture is further divided into municipalities, which consist of cities, towns, and villages.

Osaka and Kyoto are considered as urban prefectures, Hokkaido is considered as one circuit prefecture and Tokyo is considered as Metropolis.

Connectivity in Japan is highly efficient, supported by an excellent train network, comprehensive bus services, and reliable flight options.

(Giant bronze statue of Buddha Vairocana at 'Tōdai-ji', in Nara)

PROLOGUE

Welcome to Japan

Our journey began with our feet touching the ground of Narita Airport, Tokyo, awaiting us was a sleek limousine bus, our chariot to Yokohama, our home away from home.

As we disembarked from the bus, at YCAT, Yokohama, we found ourselves in the company of a young Japanese gentleman. With a hint of uncertainty, I asked, "Where is the taxi stand?"

His eyes met ours, and without a word, he took charge of the two hefty suitcases my wife was carrying. He set off at a brisk pace, leaving us in a moment of bewilderment.

With a sense of adventure, I followed him, my own suitcases in tow. We navigated the labyrinth of the bus station, riding the escalator from the east side to the west, covering a distance of almost 500 meters.

Finally, he halted at a seemingly random spot. As I caught up with him, he uttered in Japanese, "Stand here… taxi will come." The word 'Taxi' was my beacon of understanding.

A wave of relief washed over me. *I am in the right place.* And thus, our journey in the land of the rising sun began…

Welcome to Japan!

PREFACE

Many of my friends frequently inquire, "How is Japan?" Repeating the same narrative can become monotonous, which inspired me to write this book.

This work is not intended to serve as a travelogue or tour guide. Rather, it is a carefully curated compilation of insights about Japan, derived from my personal experiences and supplemented by various sources.

Myriads of books have been written about Japan, yet this book stands out by focusing on contemporary Japan, highlighting its unique characteristics and qualities.

This book is intended as a cool companion for those venturing to Japan, whether for professional endeavors or personal exploration.

Japan boasts a rich history, and the modern nation that emerged after World War II has seen remarkable development over the past ninety years. The entire nation has embraced peace and worked collectively towards the development of modern Japan. The unwavering efforts of her people have transformed Japan into one of the world's superpowers.

Preface

Japan is poised for significant changes in the coming years. The growing elderly population and declining birth rate are primary factors contributing to the workforce gap. This situation presents opportunities for foreign nationals to explore both white-collar and blue-collar employment in Japan. There is a concerted effort to evolve from a "Japanese" identity to one that is recognized as "Global."

My narrative offers insights from an Indian vantage point, avoiding comparisons between Japan and India in favor of celebrating the distinctiveness of each nation's geography, culture, and heritage. My Indian identity remains integral to my being, yet my experiences in Japan have enriched my perspective.

I present not only the commendable attributes of Japan but also its lesser-known aspects, with the understanding that no society is without its imperfections.

Lot of care has been taken to provide accurate and genuine information in this book, and some of the data are from the official websites and reliable sources.

The content herein is a fusion of my personal journey and the knowledge I have acquired, presented in simple language.

It is my sincere hope that this book serves as a valuable companion on your journey to the Land of the Rising Sun.

Japanese have learnt a lot from the past history, and it is time the rest of the world learn from Japanese. the genuine practice of "Live and Let Live."

Arigato Gozaimas (*Thank you*)

DID YOU KNOW

Swami Vivekananda's visit to Japan

Swami Vivekanand's visit was a part of his larger voyage to Chicago, where he was to represent India and Hinduism at the first World's Parliament of Religions. But instead of taking the conventional route to America, he chose to travel east, charting a course that would take him through Sri Lanka, Singapore, Hong Kong, China, and finally, Japan.

INTRODUCTION

Japan's rise to a global superpower and its ability to challenge other world powers can be attributed to several fundamental characteristics ingrained in its culture:

Cultural Values:

- Strong cultural foundation
- Preservation of historical treasures
- Love of nature
- Respect for elders
- Strong moral standards
- Cleanliness
- Patriotism

Social Characteristics:

- Ever-smiling people
- Modest home life
- Strong family values
- Honesty
- Helpfulness
- Integrity
- Inclusivity for differently abled individuals and elders
- Gender equality and women empowerment

Government and Organization:

- Benevolent government
- Comprehensive insurance coverage
- Excellent organization
- Business cooperation
- Exceptionally low crime rate

Education and Innovation:

- Compulsory education
- Technological innovation
- High discipline
- Activeness and agility

In Japan, individuals tend to mind their own business, whether in public, at work, or at home. Gender equality is evident throughout society. The country is known for its low pollution levels, environmental care, lack of adulteration, and low crime rates.

However, like any nation, Japan has its challenges:

Challenges:

- Language: Limited proficiency in languages other than Japanese.
- Taxes: High direct and indirect taxes, including substantial inheritance taxes.
- Loneliness: Increasing societal issue.
- Gadget use: High dependency on smartphones.

- Transactions: Predominance of cash transactions.
- Outdated technologies: Continued use of fax machines, CDs, DVDs, etc.
- Silence: Pervasive quietness.
- Brand consciousness: High awareness and preference for brands.

In this book, you will find reflections on Japan's unique blend of ancient traditions and cutting-edge modernity. From the serene beauty of cherry blossoms in spring to the bustling energy of Tokyo's neon-lit streets, Japan offers a fascinating tapestry of cultural experiences.

Explore the meticulous art of tea ceremonies, the elegance of traditional kimonos, and the profound philosophy behind Zen gardens. This compilation aims to provide a deeper understanding of Japan's rich cultural heritage and contemporary lifestyle.

let us explore the land of rising Sun…

IMPORTANT TELEPHONE NUMBERS IN JAPAN

"Upon arriving in any country, my foremost priority is to meticulously document essential telephone numbers that may prove invaluable in emergency situations."

1. Police: Dial 110.

   Use this number to report a crime or accident. Provide details such as the incident's location, your name, and contact information. Wait until the operator hangs up first and do not move locations until the police arrive.
2. Fire/Ambulance: Dial 119.

   For fire or medical emergencies, call 119. If you're unsure whether you need an ambulance, call #7119. Learn basic Japanese phrases like "火事です" (kaji desu) for fire and "救急" (Kyūkyū) for an ambulance. Ambulances and fire trucks are free of charge but use them responsibly.
3. Coast Guard: Dial 118.

   Contact the Japanese Coast Guard in case of trouble at sea within Japanese waters.
4. Disaster Safety Confirmation: Dial 171.

During disasters (like earthquakes), use the Disaster Line to record a voice message. Friends or family will be automatically notified.

5. Report Child Abuse: Dial 189.
   Use this emergency number to report child abuse.

Remember:

- 110 and 119 are toll-free; no need to insert coins in public phones.
- Press the red emergency button (if available) before calling.
- English is supported, but learning basic Japanese phrases is helpful.

"To be candid, Japan stands out as an exceptionally safe country, characterized by an impressively low crime rate."

DID YOU KNOW

Bodhisena – First documented Indian was a Tamil, hailing from Madurai, Tamilnadu, India.

Bodhisena, also known as Bodaisenna in Japanese, was an Indian Buddhist monk and scholar born around 704 AD in Madurai, India. He is recognized as the first documented Indian to have traveled to Japan, making a significant impact on Japanese culture and Buddhism.

Bodhisena's journey began with a mystical inspiration from Manjusri Bodhisattva, which led him to travel to China in search of the incarnation of Manjusri at Mount Wutai. While in China, he met the Japanese ambassador to the Tang court, who invited him to Japan on behalf of Emperor Shōmu. Bodhisena accepted the invitation and traveled to Japan via Cambodia and Vietnam, arriving in Osaka in 736 AD.

In Japan, Bodhisena was warmly received and played a crucial role in establishing the Kegon school of Buddhism, the Japanese transmission of the Huayan school of Chinese Buddhism. He was instrumental in teaching Sanskrit and performing significant religious ceremonies, including the eye-opening ceremony for the giant bronze statue of Buddha Vairocana at Tōdai-ji in Nara

CHAPTER 1

GETTING TO KNOW THE JAPANESE CULTURE

In Japan's embrace, traditions thrive,
A culture where the past and present jive.
From tea ceremonies, serene and slow,
To bustling cities with a vibrant glow.
Kimono's grace, in colors bright,
Sumo wrestlers' strength, a powerful sight.
Haiku poems, in nature's praise,
Cherry blossoms in springtime's haze.
Calligraphy strokes, with artful flair,
Zen gardens' peace, beyond compare.
Festivals that light the night,
With lanterns glowing, pure delight.
In every gesture, a story told,
Japanese culture, timeless and bold.
A harmony of heart and mind,
In Japan's beauty, we always find.

An Unforgettable Morning in Japan: A Tale of Cleanliness and Discipline

On the second day of our arrival, as I stepped out of my apartment, I was greeted by an unusual sight. My neighbors were diligently clearing the street, each armed with a plastic bag, picking up every bit of litter. I was intrigued by this communal act of cleanliness.

Upon inquiry, I learned that it was a daily ritual for every resident to ensure the cleanliness of the street in front of their building. The municipality's role was limited to collecting the garbage from designated locations each morning. This self-sufficient approach to cleanliness ensures that every street and road in Japan is immaculate, devoid of even a stray piece of paper.

Interestingly, dustbins are a rare sight in many public places, including railway stations. The reason? You are expected to carry your garbage home and dispose of it there. A peculiar practice, you might think, but believe me, it works. The segregation of garbage happens at home, making waste management efficient and effective.

The roots of this cleanliness ethos can be traced back to school days. Japanese children are instilled with a few fundamental values - cleanliness, discipline, individuality, and of course, a bit of academic knowledge.

One of the most remarkable aspects of Japanese culture that I've observed is the queue culture, a testament to their discipline. This orderly conduct is something I've rarely seen in many other countries I've visited. It's these unique practices that make Japan a fascinating place to experience and learn from.

A Weekend Adventure in Yokohama's Chinatown: A Tale of Lost and Found

One weekend, we set off on a shopping spree to the bustling and vibrant Chinatown in Yokohama. Our first stop was the renowned 7-eleven convenience store, a hub of diverse merchandise where I withdrew some Japanese yen to fuel our shopping expedition.

As we immersed ourselves in the shopping experience, time flew by. After nearly three hours of exploring the myriad of shops, I had a sudden realization - my mobile phone was missing. A wave of panic washed over me as I retraced my steps in my mind and concluded that I must have left it back at the 7-eleven convenience store.

With a racing heart, I dashed back to the store, hoping against hope that my phone would still be there. And to my utter surprise and relief, there it was, untouched and exactly where I had left it!

That, my friends, is the essence of Japan - a place where respect for others' belongings is deeply ingrained in the culture. It was a simple incident, but one that left a profound impression on me about *the integrity and honesty that Japan is renowned for*.

Before you set off on your adventure to Japan, a bit of preparation can make your journey smoother and more enjoyable.

Here are some tips to get you started:

Learn a few Japanese phrases: Simple greetings like "Good morning" (おはようございます – Ohayo Gozaimasu) and "Thank you" (ありがとう – Arigatou Gozaimasu) can go a long way in making connections.

Download a reliable translator app: Communication can be a challenge since English isn't widely spoken. A good app will be your best friend.

Pack season-appropriate attire: Japanese people take dressing seriously, so make sure your wardrobe is suitable for both the weather and the occasion.

Familiarize yourself with Japanese culture and etiquette: Understanding local customs will help you navigate social situations with ease.

Medication: Carry sufficient medicines as it is not that easy to get scheduled drugs in Japan.

Bring plenty of yen and an international card: Having enough local currency and a backup payment method is essential.

Let us briefly look at some essential etiquettes to observe while in Japan.

In Japan, hugs and handshakes are out, and bowing is in! It's the go-to greeting that shows respect and politeness.

Silence is golden in Japan. Whether you're in the office, on a train, or at the movies, you'll notice it's super quiet. No phone calls or loud chatter—just the natural sounds around you. If people do talk, it's usually in hushed tones.

One thing you'll admire about Japan is their love for queuing. You'll see neat lines everywhere—at train stations, elevators, eateries—you name it. If there's more than one person, a queue magically forms!

Privacy is a big deal here. The Japanese aren't fans of people invading their personal space, so it's best to avoid unnecessary chit-chat.

Remember to use "Sumimasen" (excuse me) and "Arigatou Gozaimasu" (thank you) often—they love it!

Trash bins are rare in public places, so carry your trash home with you. It's a good idea to bring a small trash bag wherever you go.

Tipping? Not in Japan! And never count your change in front of others—it's considered rude.

Jaywalking is a no-no. Always use pedestrian crossings and obey traffic signals.

If you're not confident with chopsticks, just ask for a fork or spoon. And never misuse chopsticks—it's frowned upon.

Japanese toilets are high-tech wonders! Google how to use them before you go. Even public restrooms are spotless.

Smoking is only allowed in designated areas. Carry a compact ashtray for your cigarette butts. Eating and smoking while walking is bad manners.

Say "Kanpai!" when clinking glasses before drinking—it's the Japanese way to toast.

Vending machines are everywhere and offer everything from ice cream cones to fresh juices. Learn how to use them—they're super convenient!

Vegetarianism is a bit of a mystery here. If you're vegetarian, ask for simple dishes like noodle soup or plain sandwiches. Convenience stores like 7-Eleven, My Basket, and Lawson have vegetarian options too.

For non-vegetarians, Japan is a food paradise! You'll find delicious fish, pork, beef, chicken, and more. Fried food is rare; steamed dishes are the favorite (sometimes even raw!).

Public transport is excellent—rely on it instead of taxis.

Japan is all about the STAMP culture! You can snag cool stamps at railway stations (Eki Stamp), iconic landmarks, and even temples (Goshuin stamp). Stamp books are your ticket to this adventure, and you can find them online or at stationery shops. If you're up for some stamp-collecting fun, grab a book before you head out! Only at temples, they charge a small amount for the stamp, other places it is mostly free of cost.

When visiting places of worship, learn the basic etiquette (details are in the later part of this book).

And finally, always keep smiling in public—don't be too serious!

Before traveling to Japan, it is advisable to familiarize yourself with the immigration regulations, particularly regarding prohibited items. Failure to do so may result in difficulties upon arrival, as the authorities are very strict in enforcing these rules.

Japan's immigration process is highly efficient, typically taking around 20 minutes. Have all documents ready and consider using the Google Translate app.

Upon arrival, two essentials are a SIM card and a SUICA card (train pass)

National Health Insurance

Japan's National Health Insurance (NHI) scheme is a comprehensive system designed to provide affordable healthcare to all residents, including foreign nationals living in Japan for three months or more

Key Features:

- Eligibility: All Japanese citizens and foreign residents who are not covered by other insurance plans must enroll in NHI
- Benefits: The scheme covers a wide range of medical services, including hospital visits, surgeries, and dental care. It ensures low-cost medical treatment, with a copayment system to limit out-of-pocket expenses
- Copayment Rates:
- Children under 6: 20%
- Ages 6 to 69: 30%
- Ages 70 to 74: 20% (30% for high-income earners)
- Ages 75 and above: 10%

Additional Information:

- Application: You can apply for NHI at your local city or town office. The head of the household is responsible for paying the NHI tax
- Income Declaration: Your previous year's income may need to be declared to determine the amount of NHI tax

This system ensures that everyone has access to necessary medical care, promoting overall public health and well-being.

DID YOU KNOW

Rabindranath Tagore

Rabindranath Tagore had a profound connection with Japan, visiting the country five times. His first visit in 1916 left a lasting impression on him. Tagore admired Japanese art and culture, particularly their deep affinity with nature. He stayed at the Sankeien Gardens in Yokohama, where he was inspired by the natural beauty and tranquility.

Tagore's interactions with Japanese intellectuals and artists influenced his work, and he incorporated Japanese aesthetics into his poetry. However, he was also critical of Japan's growing nationalism and imperialism. His experiences in Japan contributed to his broader vision of Pan-Asianism, advocating for unity and cultural exchange among Asian nations.

Memorize the following words to get instantly connected with Japanese

English Phrase	Japanese Equivalent
Good afternoon	こんにちは (Konnichiwa)
Good evening	こんばんは (Konbanwa)
Thank you	ありがとう (Arigatou)
Excuse me	すみません (Sumimasen)
Sorry	ごめんなさい (Gomen nasai)
How are you	お元気ですか (Ogenki desu ka)
Pleased to meet you	はじめまして (Hajimemashite)
You are most welcome	どういたしまして (Dou itashimashite)
Bye	さようなら (Sayounara)
See you	またね (Matane)
Railway station	駅 (Eki)
Bank	銀行 (Ginkou)
Where is the restaurant	レストランはどこですか (Resutoran wa doko desu ka)
What is the price of this	これはいくらですか (Kore wa ikura desu ka)
Where is the railway station	駅はどこですか (Eki wa doko desu ka)

English Phrase	Japanese Equivalent
Hot udon soup please	熱いうどんをください (Atsui udon wo kudasai)
Yes	はい (Hai)
No	いいえ (Iie)
English	英語 (Eigo)
Indian	インド人 (Indo-jin)

CHAPTER 2

GETTING TO KNOW THE JAPANESE CORPORATE CULTURE

Order and respect,
Harmony in every task,
Unity at work.

It took me three months to crack the code of Japanese office culture, and wow, it's a whole new world compared to where I've worked before!

First off, silence is golden. We're talking pin-drop silence—no mobiles ringing or vibrating, and definitely no unnecessary wandering around.

Meetings? They start on time and end on time. Punctuality is the name of the game.

Everyone is glued to their monitors. When they say they work eight hours, they really mean it!

When someone (employee) enters the office, you'll hear a hearty "Ohayo Gozaimasu" (Good morning), and when they leave, it's a loud "Mata Ashita" (See you tomorrow).

The day kicks off with Rajio Taiso exercises—a fun five-minute stretching routine to get everyone energized.

Hierarchy is a big deal here, but there's no cabin culture. Even the project director sits at an open cubicle desk. Only the board of directors get the luxury of cabins.

Nothing is free in the office. You need to bring your own coffee or tea and use the hot water in the pantry. For other beverages and snacks, hit up the vending machine.

And guess what? There's no gender bias or any other kind of bias here. Everyone's treated equally, whether it's about gender, nationality, or language.

Employees are encouraged to take leave either prefixing or suffixing the weekends. Two long holidays are famous in Japan (Golden week holidays in the month of May and New year eve in Dec/Jan).

The aging working population in Japan has led to a significant number of employees over the age of 70 still active in the workforce. This situation, coupled with the country's declining birth rate, presents a major challenge for Japan.

These demographic shifts create favorable conditions for foreign nationals to access more employment opportunities in Japan.

Afternoon powernap at office

At precisely noon, the office plunges into darkness. The lights, like punctual clockwork, retreat until 1:00 PM.

Behold the venerable Japanese tradition: the midday power nap. Employees sprawl across their desks, embracing a brief respite.

Initially, I stumbled into this twilight zone, disoriented, and clutching my coffee mug like a lifeline. But now? Oh, now I'm a seasoned power-napper. I've mastered the art of midday siestas, and let me tell you, it's like hitting the "refresh" button on my brain.

Immediately after the powernap, everyone goes to the rest room and start brushing their teeth. (It is advisable to keep a toothbrush and toothpaste in your desk). I really don't know whether this is a good habit or not, but it is their culture.

Office parties

Office parties in Japan are a delightful tradition where everyone pitches in and spends the evening together, whether it's to welcome a new colleague or bid someone farewell. These gatherings follow a fascinating fixed agenda that adds to their charm.

First, the party in charge will declare the party open, and the beer will start flowing.

I had a rather unforgettable experience at one of these parties.

As I began pouring beer into my glass, my colleague sitting next to me suddenly grabbed my hand. Confused, I asked, "Why?" He explained that in Japan, it's customary for the person next to you to fill your drink. Pouring your own drink is considered rude.

This was a completely new experience for me! My glass eventually emptied, and I found myself staring at the beer bottle, unsure of what to do. Thankfully, within minutes, my colleague noticed and filled my glass. This practice, I realized, helps control the amount of alcohol consumed. Clever, right?

Next, the food starts arriving, dish after delicious dish.

Now, it's time for the party in charge to deliver a short speech. This is followed by the serving of traditional Japanese liquors like sake and shochu. After that, you can choose your favorite drink. Don't forget to say "Kanpai" (Cheers) and clink glasses with your neighbors! 🥂

Finally, enjoy the dessert and leave the premises. And remember, never ever attempt to drive after drinking in Japan. It's considered a serious crime.

How to Rock the Japanese Corporate Scene

Never ever raise your voice nor argue, they do not like that. Explain politely your stand.

Keep Your Promises: Be the reliable superstar who always delivers. But remember, don't bite off more than you can chew!

Know Your Limits: Take on tasks that match your superpowers. Overloading yourself is a no-go.

Be Punctual: Time is precious, so be the early bird who catches the worm.

Stay Polite and Smile: A friendly smile goes a long way in brightening up the office vibe.

Dress to Impress: Formal wear is your go-to, including those snazzy shoes. (IT folks, you might have a bit more leeway!)

Color Code: Blue or black trousers and white shirts are the office favorites. Rock these colors and blend right in.

Be Open: Listen up in meetings and let everyone have their say. No bossy attitudes here—equality rules!

Express Yourself: If you disagree, do it with grace. Politeness is key to keeping the peace.

Respect Workspaces: Keep the chit-chat to a minimum and let everyone focus.

Food Etiquette: Avoid smelly desk snacks. Head to the pantry or lunch hall for your meals.

Guinness World Record by a Japanese Woman

Imagine dedicating yourself to your office for an incredible 70 years...

Yasuko Tamaki, a remarkable 90-year-old from Japan, holds the Guinness World Record as the world's oldest office manager. Since 1956, she has been a steadfast presence at Sunco Industries, a trading company specializing in screws.

Despite surpassing the typical retirement age decades ago, Yasuko continues to work five days a week, diligently managing office accounts and performing various clerical tasks. Her unwavering dedication and longevity have made her a living testament to the company's history.

DID YOU KNOW

Subash Chandra Bose and Japanese connection

Subhas Chandra Bose, a prominent Indian freedom fighter, allied with Japan during World War II to seek support for India's independence. He traveled from Germany to Japan in 1943, where he took command of the Indian National Army (INA), initially formed by Indian POWs, and led by Mohan Singh. Bose's collaboration with Japan was pivotal in organizing the INA to fight against British colonial rule in India. His efforts symbolized a significant chapter in the struggle for India's freedom.

CHAPTER 3

MUST SEE TOURIST ATTRACTIONS IN JAPAN

Japan is a treasure trove of attractions, catering to every kind of traveler. Whether you're a fan of futuristic sci-fi wonders, a seeker of traditional temples and shrines, an adventurer aiming to conquer majestic mountains, or a history buff eager to explore UNESCO World Heritage sites, Japan has something special for you. So, pack your bags and get ready for an unforgettable journey tailored to your interests.

In the land where the sun rises bright, Japan's beauty shines, day, and night.

From cherry blossoms in spring's embrace, To autumn leaves in a fiery race.

Temples whisper tales of old, Mount Fuji stands, proud and bold.

City lights that dazzle and gleam, Nature's wonders, like a dream.

Ancient streets with stories to tell, Modern marvels that cast a spell.

From bustling markets to serene shores, Japan's charm forever endures.

With every season, a new delight, Japan's beauty, pure and bright.

A tapestry of culture and grace, In every corner, a magical place.

Mount Fuji

Mount Fuji, or Fujisan, is an absolute must-see and one of Japan's most iconic attractions. Just a few hours' drive from Tokyo, this sacred and active volcano stands majestically, inviting adventurers from all over the world.

I had the incredible privilege of climbing Fujisan and witnessing a breathtaking sunrise from Level 7 (Altitude of 3000 Meters) —a truly once-in-a-lifetime experience! You can easily reach up to Level 5 by car or bus, making the journey accessible for many.

The official climbing season for Fujisan's summit runs from July to September, offering a window of opportunity to conquer this legendary peak. Surrounding Fujisan, you can explore the stunning Fuji Five Lakes—Lake Kawaguchiko, Lake Yamanakako, Lake Saiko, Lake

Shojiko, and Lake Motosuko. Don't miss the famous Mt. Fuji Panoramic Ropeway for spectacular views!

Hakone, Gotemba, and Kawaguchiko are popular areas to spend time near Mount Fuji.

Mount Fuji trail opens from July till September, and I suggest you engage a guide for the trail. It is not as easy as you think if you are not a professional.

Tip: Do not miss the Onsen (Hot Springs) experience here.

Tokyo

Tokyo is brimming with incredible attractions! The towering Tokyo Sky tree (634 meters) and the iconic Tokyo Tower (333 meters) offer breathtaking views of the cityscape.

Don't miss out on the serene Ueno Park and the majestic Imperial Palace, both must-see spots in Tokyo. For those enchanted by temples and shrines, the Asakusa area is a treasure trove, home to the famous Senso-ji Temple.

Shopping enthusiasts will love the bustling Shibuya and upscale Ginza districts, which also boast numerous Japanese restaurants to tantalize your taste buds.

Tokyo Disney Resort, located in Urayasu, Chiba Prefecture, is Japan's magical gateway to Disney fun. The resort features two main theme parks: Tokyo Disneyland and Tokyo DisneySea

Tokyo Disneyland is modeled after Disneyland in California and the Magic Kingdom in Florida, offering seven themed lands filled with exciting attractions, seasonal decorations, and enchanting parades

Tokyo Disney Sea is unique to Japan, inspired by the myths and legends of the sea, with stunning themed ports and thrilling rides.

Both parks provide unforgettable experiences for visitors of all ages, making Tokyo Disney Resort a must-visit destination for Disney fans.

Many travelers overlook the vibrant city of Yokohama, just a short train ride from Tokyo (about 2 hours). I highly recommend staying in Yokohama for a more economical yet equally exciting experience.

Yokohama is packed with fantastic attractions like the futuristic Minato Mirai area, the tranquil Sankeien Garden, and the fascinating Cup Noodles Museum (thanks to Nissin, the inventor of the famous cup noodles).

Kamakura

Kamakura is similar to Kanchipuram (Tamil Nadu, INDIA) which houses wonderful temples and shrines which are centuries old. (Kanchipuram is a small city, near Chennai, INDIA, known as city of thousand Hindu temples)

Kamakura, often referred to as the "Kyoto of the East," was a significant historical city in Japan. During the Kamakura period (1185-1333), it served as the political center of Japan under the rule of the first shogun, Minamoto no Yoritomo. This era saw the rise of the samurai class and the establishment of a feudal system.

Kamakura is renowned for its impressive temples and shrines, many of which were built during this period. Notable sites include the Great Buddha (Daibutsu) at Kotoku-in Temple and the serene Zen temples like Engaku-ji and Kencho-ji. The city also played a crucial role in the spread of Zen Buddhism in Japan.

Surrounded by mountains and the sea, Kamakura offers a blend of natural beauty and historical significance, making it a fascinating destination for those interested in Japan's rich cultural heritage.

Tip: Don't miss out the Samurai/Yukata attire and Kimono attire here. There are many shops which rent them out for taking photographs.

Hiroshima and Miyajima Island

Who can forget the harrowing events of the atomic bombing of Hiroshima during WWII? Visiting the Hiroshima Peace Memorial is a deeply moving experience that might keep you up at night, reflecting on its profound history.

Yet, the resilience of Hiroshima is nothing short of remarkable. This beautiful city, steeped in traditional Japanese culture, has risen from the ashes. Here, cabbage is revered almost like a deity, often served free as a salad in many restaurants. This humble vegetable was crucial for survival in the aftermath of the bombing.

Don't miss trying Hiroshima's famous okonomiyaki, a savory pancake that's a local culinary delight.

Just a short trip away, Miyajima Island awaits with its stunning natural beauty. The island is home to the iconic Itsukushima Shrine, known for its "floating" torii gate. A visit to Miyajima is a must, as it offers a rich tapestry of history and breathtaking scenery.

Kansai Trio: Osaka, Kyoto, and Nara

Osaka, Kyoto, and Nara are often referred to as the Kansai Trio. These cities are close to each other and well-connected by public transportation, making it easy to travel between them.

Kyoto is known for its rich history, ancient temples, and beautiful gardens.

Nara is famous for its friendly deer and the impressive Todai-ji Temple, which houses one of the largest bronze Buddha statues in Japan.

Osaka is a vibrant city known for its modern architecture, nightlife, and delicious street food

Kyoto has always held a special place in my heart as Japan's cultural capital. Before Tokyo took the spotlight, Kyoto was the nation's capital, overflowing with history and charm. While Kamakura also boasts stunning temples, Kyoto's magnificent shrines truly steal the show.

Don't miss the iconic Ginkaku-ji and Kinkaku-ji temples in Kyoto, known as the Silver Pavilion and Golden Pavilion. Their names reflect their dazzling beauty, with "Gin" meaning silver and "Kin" meaning gold.

Toyama and Fukui

Toyama, nestled in Japan's Chubu region, is a paradise for nature lovers and hiking enthusiasts. The area is renowned for its breathtaking landscapes, including the majestic Tateyama mountain Range. One of the most popular trails is the Tateyama Kurobe Alpine Route, which offers stunning views of rugged mountains, crystal-clear rivers, and lush forests.

Whether you're a seasoned hiker or just looking for a scenic walk, Toyama's trails, such as the Mikurigaike Pond Loop and the challenging ascent to Mount Tsurugi, provide unforgettable experiences. Each season brings its own unique beauty, from vibrant autumn leaves to serene snow-covered peaks

Eiheiji Temple: Founded in 1244, this Zen temple is known for its serene beauty and tranquil surroundings. Visitors can explore the temple's various buildings and gardens, and even participate in Zen practices through a one-night stay program.

Fukui Prefectural Dinosaur Museum: One of the largest dinosaur museums in the world, this museum features cutting-edge exhibits and educational programs, making it a must-visit for dinosaur enthusiasts.

Nagasaki

Nagasaki, a city rich in history and culture, offers a captivating experience for tourists. Start your journey at the Nagasaki Peace Park and Atomic Bomb Museum, where you can reflect on the city's poignant past.

Explore the charming Glover Garden, which highlights Western-style residences and offers stunning views of the harbor. Don't miss the Oura Cathedral, Japan's oldest Christian church and a UNESCO World Heritage Site.

For a taste of local life, wander through Chinatown and savor Nagasaki's famous street food. A visit to Hashima Island, also known as Gunkanjima or Battleship Island, provides a glimpse into Japan's industrial history.

Shikoku Island

Shikoku Island is my absolute favorite place in Japan, where nature truly shines at its best. Nestled within a stunning mountain range and home to four prefectures—Tokushima, Kochi, Ehime, and Kagawa—Shikoku is renowned for its legendary 88 Temples Pilgrimage.

Kobo Daishi, also known as Kukai, is a revered figure in Japanese history and the founder of the Shingon School of Buddhism. Born in 774 in Zentsuji, Shikoku, he was a priest, scholar, artist, and engineer. Kukai traveled to China to study Buddhism and, upon his return, established the Shingon retreat on Mount Koya.

Kobo Daishi is closely associated with the Shikoku Pilgrimage, a journey of 88 temples that he is believed to have either founded or visited. This pilgrimage attracts many who seek spiritual growth, healing, and a deeper connection with nature.

This famous pilgrimage, deeply rooted in Japanese culture, spans approximately 1,200 kilometers, and takes around 60 days to complete on foot.

So far, I've had the incredible experience of visiting 20 of these sacred temples. Each step of the journey offers a serene escape into unspoiled nature, with lush greenery and pristine air all around.

Kagawa, one of the prefectures on Shikoku, is also celebrated for its delicious 'udon noodles.' These thick, chewy noodles are a must-try for any visitor, offering a taste of local culinary tradition.

Whether you're seeking spiritual enrichment or simply a peaceful retreat, Shikoku Island is a haven of natural beauty and cultural heritage.

Okinawa

Okinawa is a fantastic stop on your way to Shikoku, and a one-day visit is definitely worth it. The Aquarium and Castle are must-see attractions that will make your trip unforgettable.

Hokkaido

Hokkaido, Japan's northernmost island, is a haven for nature enthusiasts and adventure seekers. The region boasts stunning landscapes, from the rugged beauty of Shiretoko National Park to the serene shores of Lake Toya.

In winter, Hokkaido transforms into a snowy wonderland, perfect for skiing and snowboarding at resorts like Niseko. Summer brings vibrant flower fields in Furano and scenic hikes in Daisetsuzan National Park.

Don't miss the lively city of Sapporo, famous for its annual Snow Festival and delicious seafood. Whether you're exploring hot springs, enjoying local cuisine, or marveling at the natural beauty, Hokkaido offers unforgettable experiences year-round.

I bet you've already imagined yourself exploring all these amazing places! I hope you get to turn those dreams into reality someday.

The best time to visit Japan from India is during "spring" (March to May) and "autumn" (September to November)

Spring (March to May) – Best Season to visit Japan

Cherry Blossoms: This is the iconic Sakura season, where cherry blossoms bloom across the country, creating picturesque landscapes.

Pleasant Weather: Temperatures are mild, making it perfect for sightseeing and outdoor activities.

Festivals: Enjoy various cherry blossom festivals and traditional events like the Takayama Festival.

Autumn (September to November)

Autumn Foliage: The fall colors transform Japan's forests, gardens, and temple grounds into vibrant shades of red, orange, and gold.

Comfortable Climate: The weather is cool and sunny, ideal for exploring cities and nature.

Fewer Crowds: Compared to the cherry blossom season, autumn sees fewer tourists, allowing for a more relaxed experience

Both seasons offer unique experiences and stunning scenery, making them the best times to explore Japan.

One-week itinerary

Day 1: Arrival in Tokyo

- Morning: Land in Tokyo and check into a budget-friendly hotel or hostel.
- Afternoon: Visit Asakusa to see the famous Senso-ji Temple and explore Nakamise Shopping Street.
- Evening: Head to Shibuya Crossing and enjoy the vibrant nightlife. Don't forget to snap a photo at the iconic crossing!

Day 2: Tokyo Exploration

- Morning: Explore Meiji Shrine and take a stroll through Yoyogi Park.

- Afternoon: Visit Harajuku for some quirky fashion and delicious crepes.
- Evening: Discover Akihabara, the hub for electronics and anime. Maybe pick up a cool gadget or two!

Day 3: Day Trip to Mount Fuji

- Morning: Take a bus or train to Lake Kawaguchi for stunning views of Mount Fuji.
- Afternoon: Enjoy a boat ride on the lake and visit the Kawaguchiko Music Forest Museum.
- Evening: Return to Tokyo and relax at your accommodation.

Day 4: Tokyo to Kyoto

- Morning: Take the Shinkansen (bullet train) to Kyoto. It's fast and efficient!
- Afternoon: Check into your accommodation and visit Fushimi Inari Shrine with its famous torii gates.
- Evening: Stroll through Gion District!

Day 5: Kyoto Exploration

- Morning: Visit Kinkaku-ji (Golden Pavilion) and Ryoan-ji (Zen rock garden).
- Afternoon: Explore Arashiyama Bamboo Grove and Tenryu-ji Temple.
- Evening: Enjoy a traditional tea ceremony or visit a local izakaya for dinner.

Day 6: Kyoto to Hiroshima

– Morning: Take the Shinkansen to Hiroshima.
– Afternoon: Visit the Hiroshima Peace Memorial Park and Atomic Bomb Dome. Reflect on the history and resilience of the city.
– Evening: Explore Hiroshima's local cuisine, like okonomiyaki (savory pancakes).

Day 7: Hiroshima to Osaka

– Morning: Take a train to Osaka and check into your accommodation.
– Afternoon: Visit Osaka Castle and its beautiful gardens.
– Evening: Explore Dotonbori for amazing street food like takoyaki and okonomiyaki. Don't miss the neon lights and lively atmosphere!

Additional Tips:

– Transportation: Get a Japan Rail Pass for unlimited travel on JR trains. It's economical and convenient.
– Food: Look for budget-friendly restaurants and convenience stores for meals. Try local specialties like ramen, sushi, and tempura.
– Accommodation: Consider staying in hostels, budget hotels, or capsule hotels to save money.
– Shopping: Visit 100-yen shops for affordable souvenirs and essentials.

This itinerary covers the best of Tokyo, Kyoto, Hiroshima, and Osaka, ensuring you experience Japan's rich culture, history, and modernity without breaking the bank.

Shopping at Japan

Shopping in Japan is like a treasure hunt with a twist! You get top-notch quality at prices that won't make your wallet cry. But if you're a true bargain hunter, the flea markets and second-hand stores are where the real adventure begins.

Picture this: Flea markets are like pop-up parties where you never know what you'll find—maybe a vintage kimono or a quirky gadget you didn't know you needed. They're here today, gone tomorrow, adding a dash of excitement to your shopping spree.

On the other hand, second-hand stores are the reliable friends who are always there for you. They offer a permanent treasure trove of pre-loved goodies, from designer bags to retro video games, all waiting for a new home.

So, whether you're in the mood for a spontaneous shopping escapade or a steady stream of hidden gems, Japan's got you covered!

Tokyo offers a vibrant flea market scene where you can find a wide range of items, including electronic goods. Here are some highlights:

Popular Flea Markets

Ohi Racecourse Flea Market (Tokyo City Flea Market): One of the largest and most popular flea markets in Tokyo, held every weekend. You can find a variety of items, including second-hand electronics

Mottainai Flea Market: Known for its eco-friendly approach, this market offers a mix of goods, including electronics, at various locations around Tokyo

Shinjuku Central Park Flea Market: Located in the heart of Shinjuku, this market is a great spot for finding vintage electronics and other unique items

Akihabara Flea Market: While not a traditional flea market, Akihabara is famous for its electronics stores and occasional street markets where you can find second-hand gadgets and parts

Yoyogi Park Flea Market: Held monthly, this market offers a variety of items, including electronics. It's a great place to find unique and vintage gadgets

Second-Hand Electronics Stores

If you're specifically looking for electronic goods, Tokyo has several second-hand stores that are worth checking out:

TOKYO PC: Offers a variety of second-hand computers and related accessories

Tsukumo Pasokon Honten Reuse Kan: Focuses on reused computer parts and peripherals

Map Camera: A great place to find second-hand cameras and photography equipment

Second Street: Second Street is a popular chain with multiple locations across Tokyo. They offer a wide range of second-hand goods, including clothing, furniture, and electronics. It's a great place to find high-quality items at reasonable prices

Treasure Factory: Treasure Factory, often referred to as "TreFac," is known for its extensive selection of second-hand goods. They have several stores in Tokyo, offering everything from designer clothes to household items and electronics

BazzStore: BazzStore has multiple locations and is known for its affordable prices and wide variety of items. You can find branded clothing, accessories, and sometimes electronics. It's a great spot for bargain hunters

Kindal: Kindal specializes in second-hand designer clothing and accessories. They have several stores in Tokyo, including one in Shinjuku. It's a great place to find high-end fashion at discounted prices

Ecomesse: Ecomesse is a charity shop that operates several locations across Tokyo. They offer a range of second-hand goods, including clothes, crockery, and household items. The profits support various charitable causes

Hard Off: Hard Off is part of the Off House chain and specializes in second-hand electronics. They have multiple locations in Tokyo where you can find used gadgets, computers, and other electronic items

Janpara: Janpara is known for its extensive selection of reused PCs, smartphones, tablets, and digital cameras. It's a great place to find quality electronics at affordable prices

Shimokitazawa Area: Shimokitazawa is famous for its vintage shops and second-hand stores. You can find a variety of items, including clothing, records, and sometimes electronics. It's a great area to explore for unique finds.

These markets and stores provide excellent opportunities to find quality electronics at affordable prices.

When exploring Tokyo's flea markets, here are some specific items you might want to keep an eye out for:

Vintage Clothing

– Retro Kimonos: Beautiful traditional garments that can be both a fashion statement and a piece of art.

- Classic Denim Jackets: Timeless pieces that add a vintage touch to any wardrobe

Antique Collectibles

- Japanese Ceramics: Traditional pottery and porcelain items that are both decorative and functional.
- Rare Collectibles: Items like old coins, stamps, and vintage toys that can be unique finds

Handmade Crafts

- Local Artisans' Creations: Beautifully crafted items such as jewelry, pottery, and textiles that showcase local talent

Electronics

- Vintage Cameras: Classic film cameras that are popular among photography enthusiasts.
- Second-Hand Gadgets: Items like used smartphones, tablets, and laptops that can be found at a fraction of the original price

Miscellaneous

- Vinyl Records: For music lovers, finding rare and vintage records can be a real treasure.
- Books and Manga: Second-hand books and manga are often available at great prices

These items not only offer great value but also provide a glimpse into Japan's rich culture and history.

DID YOU KNOW

"Love in Tokyo" is a classic Indian movie released in 1966, starring Joy Mukherjee and Asha Parekh. It was known for its hit song "Sayonara Sayonara," which introduced many Indians to the Japanese word for farewell. The movie was shot in various locations around Tokyo, including Hibiya Park, the Imperial Palace, Haneda Airport, Tokyo Monorail, Tokyo Tower, Zozoji Temple grounds, and the Ginza shopping district

CHAPTER 5

JAPANESE DELICACIES AND DRINKS

In Japan's kitchens, a symphony plays,
Of flavors and textures, in countless ways.
Sushi rolls crafted with delicate care,
Fresh fish and rice, a perfect pair.

Ramen bowls steaming, rich broth so deep,
Noodles that comfort, in every slurp we keep.
Okonomiyaki, savory pancake delight,
A taste of Osaka, in every bite.

Tempura's crunch, a golden delight,
Vegetables and shrimp, fried just right.
Ton-katsu crispy, pork cutlet's charm,
A hearty meal, that keeps us warm.

Savor the umami in miso's embrace,
A warm, hearty soup, a taste to chase.

Onigiri, rice balls, simple and neat,
A portable snack, that's hard to beat.

Takoyaki balls, with octopus inside,
Street food joy, in every bite we find.
Shojin ryori, monk's vegan fare,
A spiritual feast, beyond compare.

Sashimi slices, pure and clean,
A taste of the ocean, fresh and serene.
Matcha green tea, a bitter-sweet blend,
A calming ritual, from start to end.

From bento boxes, artfully arranged,
To kaiseki feasts, meticulously staged.
Japanese cuisine, a culinary art,
A journey of flavors, that warms the heart.

Welcome to Japan, the ultimate paradise for your taste buds! With a dazzling array of dishes, each boasting its own unique flair, you'll be in culinary heaven.

Pro tip: Master the art of chopsticks! If you're not yet a chopstick ninja, hop onto YouTube and learn the ropes. Trust me, the Japanese take chopstick etiquette seriously, and you don't want to disrespect the delicious food.

And here's a fun fact: slurping your soup is totally cool! Feel free to lift your bowl and enjoy every last drop Savoring the Flavors.

A Culinary Journey Through Japan

Where Rice Meets Raw Fish and Perfection Blooms

Japan, a land where culinary artistry dances on the taste buds, beckons food enthusiasts from every corner of the globe. Whether you're a seasoned sushi connoisseur or a curious foodie, Japan's gastronomic offerings promise an unforgettable adventure.

So, grab your chopsticks and let's explore the delicacies that make Japan a food lover's paradise! – My Top 10 picks...

1. Sushi: A Symphony of Simplicity
   Sushi, the iconic Japanese dish, is more than just raw fish on vinegared rice. It's a harmonious blend of flavors, textures, and tradition. Imagine delicate slices of maguro (tuna), buttery salmon, and sweet ebi (shrimp) atop perfectly seasoned rice. Each bite is a celebration—a miniature firework display in your mouth. And if you're feeling adventurous, try uni (sea urchin) or tamago (sweet omelette) for a taste of sushi heaven.

2. Okonomiyaki: Pancakes with Personality
   Okonomiyaki, often dubbed "Japanese savory pancakes," are like edible mood rings. These fluffy delights are customizable—mix shredded cabbage, batter, and your favorite ingredients (think shrimp, pork, or squid). Then, grill them to crispy perfection. Top with okonomiyaki sauce, mayo, bonito flakes, and seaweed. The result? A savory symphony that sings "comfort food" in every bite.
3. Takoyaki: Octopus Balls of Joy
   Takoyaki—tiny, round, and irresistible. Picture a street vendor expertly flipping these golden orbs in a sizzling pan. Inside, you'll find tender chunks of octopus, scallions, and a secret blend of spices. Drizzle with takoyaki sauce, sprinkle with seaweed, and pop them into your mouth. The burst of umami will leave you craving more.
4. Bento: Lunchbox Magic
   Bento, the Japanese lunchbox, is a work of art. It's not just about sustenance; it's about aesthetics. Imagine neatly arranged compartments filled with rice, pickled vegetables, grilled fish, and tamagoyaki (rolled omelette). Each bite tells a story—a taste of home, a hint of nostalgia. And don't forget the kawaii (cute) character-shaped bento boxes that make lunchtime an adventure!

5. Tempura: Crispy Elegance
Tempura is the epitome of elegance. Fresh seafood and vegetables are lightly battered and fried to crispy perfection. Dip them in tentsuyu (dipping sauce) and savor the delicate crunch. From prawns to sweet potatoes, tempura transcends mere fried food—it's a culinary ballet.
6. Udon Noodles: Slurp-Worthy Satisfaction
Udon noodles are thick, chewy, and oh-so-satisfying. Imagine a steaming bowl of these wheat-based wonders swimming in a fragrant broth. Add tempura bits, green onions, and a sprinkle of shichimi (seven-spice blend). The slurping etiquette? Simple: the louder, the better!
7. Tonkatsu: Pork Cutlet Perfection
Tonkatsu—a crispy breaded pork cutlet that's a symphony of crunch. Dip it in tonkatsu sauce, and you'll understand why it's a comfort food classic. Pair it with shredded cabbage and a side of miso soup for a balanced meal.
8. Onigiri: Rice Balls Wrapped in Love
Onigiri, those adorable rice triangles, are the ultimate portable snack. Stuffed with pickled plum, salmon, or spicy cod roe, they're wrapped in nori (seaweed) like a cozy blanket. Perfect for picnics, train rides, or midnight cravings.

9. Curry: Japan's Comfort Blanket
   Japanese curry is a hug in a bowl. It's thicker, sweeter, and less spicy than its Indian counterpart. Picture tender chunks of meat (or veggies) swimming in a velvety curry sauce. Pour it over rice, and you're home.
10. Ramen: Noodles with Soul
    Ramen, the soul-soothing noodle soup, deserves a standing ovation. Whether it's tonkotsu (pork bone broth), miso, or shoyu (soy sauce), each bowl is a masterpiece. Slurp those noodles, sip that broth, and let the umami transport you to nirvana.

Japanese drinks

Sake: The Rice Wine Odyssey Sake's story begins around 2500 years ago, when the technique to ferment rice into an alcoholic drink was developed in ancient China. This boozy wisdom traveled to Japan along with rice cultivation, and the Japanese, being the perfectionists they are, refined it to create what we now know as sake.

Imagine ancient Japanese folks, after a hard day's work in the rice fields, sitting down and thinking, "How can we make this grain more… entertaining?" And thus, sake was born. It was first mentioned in the 3rd century, and by the 8th century, they were using mold (koji) to brew it. Fast forward to the 1600s, and sake production became an industry, with Itami earning its stars as a sake producer.

The 20th century brought about the first export of sake, and the National Research Institute of Brewing started handing out annual awards like it was Oscar season for liquors. But like any good drama, there was a twist: war-related food shortages in the 1940s limited sake production. Yet, sake survived, and today, it's not just a drink; it's a cultural icon.

Shochu: The Distilled Delight Shochu, on the other hand, is the younger, feistier sibling, starting production about 500 years ago in southern Japan. It's the result of a happy marriage between the basic sake brewing technique and the distillation method.

The distillation technique was like the new kid on the block, arriving in Japan around the 15th century through trade with surrounding countries. The oldest domestic record of shochu dates back to 1546, when a Portuguese merchant noted that people were enjoying a rice spirit in the Yamagawa area.

Shochu was the drink of the people, and by the 16th century, it had become deeply ingrained in Japanese culture, reflecting regional traditions and preferences. It's like the versatile actor of spirits, distilled from anything from rice to sweet potatoes to even carrots!

So, there you have it, the spirited saga of sake and shochu. One, a refined classic that's been the life of the party for millennia; the other, a bold upstart that's not afraid to mix it up. Both have shaped Japan's history, one sip at a time.

Japanese Whisky

Inspiration: Modeled after Scottish tradition.

Ingredients: Double-distilled from malted barley, aged in oak casks (including Japanese Mizunara oak).

History: Official production began in 1923 at the Yamazaki distillery.

Notable Distilleries: Yamazaki, Suntory, Kirin, and Nikka.

Two best whiskies of Japan

Yamazaki is Japan's first and oldest malt whisky distillery, founded in 1923 by Shinjiro Torii. Nestled at the foot of Mt. Tennozan, southwest of Kyoto, this distillery is the birthplace of Japanese whisky.

Hibiki Whisky: Hibiki, meaning "resonance," is a harmonious blend of malt and grain whiskies, meticulously crafted by the House of Suntory.

Both these whiskies are expensive, and many economical brands are available at all leading stores. Kirin and Suntory are famous brands for beer.

Themed bars in Japan

Japan is home to a plethora of unique and creatively themed bars that cater to various interests. Whether you're into quirky decor, immersive experiences, or just want something out of the ordinary, here are some fascinating themed bars you might enjoy:

Bacon (Shin-Okubo, Tokyo):

Inspired by artist Damien Hirst's 'Pharmacy' installation, Bacon features neon lights, plastic stools, and a vibe reminiscent of an art gallery. The name pays homage to both the family business downstairs (a samgyeopsal restaurant) and the painter Francis Bacon

Gen Yamamoto (Azabu-Juban, Tokyo):

A cocktail sanctuary where mixologist Gen Yamamoto crafts exquisite cocktails using domestically sourced fruits and vegetables. Instead of a menu, customers select a tasting set of four to seven cocktails, each individually served with ingredients explained.

Albatross Bar (Golden Gai, Shinjuku, Tokyo):

Located in the historic Golden Gai district, Albatross Bar is a cozy spot with a retro vibe. It's a great place to experience the nostalgic charm of old Tokyo while sipping on drinks.

Penguin Bar Ikebukuro (Ikebukuro, Tokyo):

Yes, you read that right! This bar is home to real penguins. Enjoy your drinks in the company of these adorable flightless birds. It's a truly unique experience.

The Lockup (Various locations):

Step into a jail cell-themed bar with crime-inspired cocktails. The staff dress as prison guards, and the ambiance is eerie yet fun. It's like being in a haunted house while enjoying your drinks.

Bar Ginza Panorama (Tokyo):

If you're a train enthusiast, this small-scale train spotting bar is a must-visit. Sip your drink while watching miniature trains zip around the tracks.

Remember that these bars often have limited seating, so it's a good idea to check their hours and make reservations if possible. Enjoy your late-night adventures in Japan's unique and unforgettable bars...

Being a veggie in Japan

Being a vegetarian in Japan is totally doable, but it does require a bit of awareness and planning. Here are some tips to help you navigate your veggie journey:

Communication:

– Learn basic Japanese phrases related to vegetarianism. For example:

– "Watashi wa bejitarian desu" (I am a vegetarian).

– "Yasai dake onegaishimasu" (Only vegetables, please).

"Niku wa tabemasen" (肉は食べません) - This means "I don't eat meat."

You can also say:

"Niku nashi de onegaishimasu" (肉なしでお願いします) - This means "Without meat, please."

– Use translation apps or carry a pocket guide with common phrases. Trust me, Google Translate will be your best friend!

Dining Options:

– Tokyo and other major cities have a growing number of vegetarian and vegan restaurants. Look for these keywords:

- Shojin Ryori: Traditional Buddhist vegetarian cuisine.
- Vegetarian (ベジタリアン) or Vegan (ビーガン) signs.
- Indian and Middle Eastern restaurants often have vegetarian options. Curry, anyone?
- Explore local markets and supermarkets for fresh fruits, vegetables, and snacks. You might discover some quirky Japanese veggies!

Sushi and Ramen:

- Sushi: Opt for vegetable sushi (nigiri) or rolls (maki) with cucumber, avocado, or pickled radish. Who knew sushi could be so green?
- Ramen: Some ramen shops offer vegetarian versions. Just ask for "yasai ramen" and slurp away!

Tempura:

- Tempura (battered and fried vegetables) is a popular dish. Make sure the dipping sauce (tentsuyu) is vegetarian. Because who doesn't love fried veggies?

Convenience Stores:

- Convenience stores (like 7-Eleven and FamilyMart) have vegetarian options:
- Onigiri (rice balls) with pickled plum or seaweed fillings.

– Salads, fruit cups, and vegetable snacks. Perfect for a quick bite!

Bento Boxes:

– Look for bento boxes with vegetable-based sides. Some train stations have vegetarian-friendly ekiben (boxed meals). Train travel and tasty food? Yes, please!

Traditional Tea Houses:

– Visit tea houses in Kyoto for matcha (green tea) and wagashi (traditional sweets). Some tea houses offer vegetarian options. Time for a zen moment!

Accommodations:

– Inform your hotel or ryokan about your dietary preferences in advance. Many hotels offer vegetarian breakfasts. Start your day the veggie way!

Learn About Ingredients:

– Familiarize yourself with common Japanese ingredients:
– Dashi: A fish-based broth used in many dishes. Ask for vegetarian dashi alternatives.
– Seaweed: Often used in soups and salads.
– Tofu: A staple in Japanese cuisine. Tofu party, anyone?

– Miso: Vegetarian miso soup is widely available. Warm and comforting!

Be Flexible and Polite:

– While Japan is becoming more vegetarian-friendly, some traditional dishes may not have vegetarian versions. Be patient and respectful when communicating your dietary needs. A smile goes a long way!

DID YOU KNOW

Lucky numbers and unlucky numbers of Japanese

Lucky numbers

7 - Shintoism: The Indigenous religion of Japan, Shinto, recognizes *seven* lucky gods, known as Shichifukujin, who are believed to bring good fortune and blessings.

8 - Another number considered lucky in Japan is 8 (八, hachi), largely because its shape (八) widens at the bottom, symbolizing growth and prosperity spreading into the future.

Unlucky numbers

4 (四, shi): This number is avoided because it sounds like the word for death (死, shi). It's common to see the fourth floor omitted in hospitals or hotels, and gifts are not given in sets of four.

9 (九, ku): Similarly, the number nine is considered unlucky because it sounds like the word for suffering or agony (苦, ku). As with the number four, rooms or floors numbered nine may be skipped in buildings.
42: Pronounced as "shi-ni," which can mean "to death", and is often avoided in contexts like car racing numbers.
49: Pronounced as "shi-ku," which can be interpreted as "painful death" or "suffering till death", and is also avoided.
43 is considered taboo, especially in maternity wards, as it can mean "stillbirth" (死産, shizan: 死 - death/to die and 産 - childbirth/produce)

CHAPTER 6

COURTEOUS JAPANESE

(Real life experience)

Lanterns softly glow,
Festivals light up the night,
Joy in every heart.

Upon our arrival in Yokohama, we alighted from the taxi and made our way into the apartment complex. Detailed instructions were provided for retrieving the key from the mailbox—a task that proved to be quite the endeavor, consuming over thirty minutes of concerted effort before we finally succeeded.

Once inside the apartment, we encountered the next set of challenges: navigating the sensor-controlled electrical consoles and appliances. The apartment was fully furnished, and all the instructions were meticulously organized, yet they were entirely in Japanese, which posed a significant barrier.

Despite these initial hurdles, we managed to settle in on our first day, even preparing our own dinner.

The following morning, we were greeted by an unexpected knock on the door. To our surprise, a Japanese gentleman stood there, checklist in hand. He proceeded to inventory each item within the apartment, his English fragmented yet sufficient for the task at hand, and he even included the hand towels in his meticulous review. (I was wondering how I am going to return the hand towels after few years of stay?)

He later explained that upon our departure, a maintenance team would inspect the apartment once more, ensuring nothing was amiss or damaged.

The apartment featured wooden flooring, which he instructed us on how to maintain. Although his approach was somewhat stern, he was ultimately amiable and helpful.

One commendable aspect of the apartment's maintenance was the routine safety checks conducted every six months, including inspections of the fire alarm, sprinklers, smoke detectors, and cleaning of the air conditioner. The advanced sensor-controlled gas stove was also noteworthy.

The only drawback was the compact size of the rooms. Accustomed to more spacious accommodations, we initially found the transition challenging. My wife humorously referred to it as a "matchbox apartment," but in time, we grew to appreciate its efficient design.

On the second day in Japan, I had two crucial missions: first, to register at the Minami Ward office, and second, to open a bank account.

When I arrived at the ward office, I was absolutely floored. It felt like stepping into a sleek corporate headquarters, nothing like the typical government offices back in India. The receptionist greeted me with a warm smile, and the entire registration process was wrapped up in a swift 30 minutes. Everything was so systematic and meticulous—it was like clockwork!

The next day, I set off for the bank. SMBC's office was colossal, with front doors that looked like they belonged to a fortress—15 feet high and 10 feet wide! I got there at 9:30 AM, eagerly waiting for the doors to open. As time ticked by, more people arrived, forming a neat queue. This is one aspect of Japanese culture that I truly admire—queuing is practically in their DNA.

At exactly 10 AM, the doors swung open, and to my amazement, the entire bank staff lined up behind them, greeting us with smiles and a cheerful "Welcome!" I was blown away; I'd never experienced such a reception before. My account opening was completed in a mere 15 minutes, and this memory remains vivid and fresh in my mind to this day.

On a rainy evening, we strolled down one of the calmest streets near my home. The gentle patter of raindrops created a serene atmosphere, perfect for a quiet walk. As we wandered, we stumbled upon a quaint little shop run by an elderly couple, who must have been in their eighties. They sold antiques and used articles, each item carrying a story of its own.

We found a beautiful Buddha statue and, after a pleasant exchange, bought it for a good deal. This experience highlighted a beautiful aspect of Japanese culture: nothing goes to waste. Everything, including books, is cherished, and passed on. Although I don't frequent used bookstores due to the language barrier, we became regular visitors to this charming shop. The smiles on the old couple's faces whenever we visited warmed my heart.

One day, a particular item caught my eye—a commemorative coin of the 1964 Tokyo Olympics, made of 99.9% silver. As a numismatist, I was thrilled. I asked the old man, "Ikura desu ka?" He gently replied that it wasn't for sale; it was a cherished possession of his. Disappointed, I nodded and began to leave. But then, he called me back, handed me the coin, and said keep it. I was stunned and asked how much I should pay. He simply smiled and said, "Nothing, just keep it as my gift."

I couldn't believe our luck and excitedly told my wife about the rare coin. Two weeks later, we returned to the shop, only to find it closed. We inquired at the neighboring store and learned that the *old couple had sold the shop and returned to their native village*. It felt like losing a part of our family. However, we had taken a selfie with the couple, a cherished memory of our time in Japan, and a reminder of the kindness we experienced.

Japanese treat their customers as king. This is one unique feature of Japanese culture.

One fine day, India ceased exporting rice, leading to a shortage of Indian rice in Japan. We seldom eat Japanese rice due to its sticky nature. When we contacted our regular supplier, he regretfully informed us that there was no stock of Indian rice and he had no idea when it would be available again.

Fortunately, a friend living near Kawasaki mentioned that Indian rice was available at a specific Asian grocery shop. Without hesitation, we rushed there in the evening and managed to buy a sizable quantity. As we were returning home, we found ourselves stuck at a station, unsure of the route to the subway train. We asked the station master for directions, and he kindly guided us to one exit. However, even after reaching the exit, we were still unclear about the route.

We spotted two young Japanese girls and asked them how to get to the subway. With warm smiles, they said, “Please follow us.” To our amazement, the subway was almost a kilometer away, yet they graciously led us there, showed us the entrance, and then smiled again before walking back.

We were stunned and couldn’t believe the kindness we had just experienced. It reminded us of our first day in Japan when a gentleman had guided us to the taxi stand. Courtesy seems to be ingrained in their culture. This heartwarming incident is one that I will never forget.

When embarking on our tours to enchanting destinations like Osaka, Kyoto, Hiroshima, and Kamakura, we always pack our trusty selfie stand. Yet, despite its convenience, there’s a limitation: time.

With so much to explore, we often find ourselves racing against the clock to cover every nook and cranny of these captivating tourist attractions.

But then, something magical happens. Everywhere we go, the locals—often gracious ladies—step forward, their smiles warm and genuine. They offer to capture our moments against the backdrop of these iconic places. It’s a selfless act, one that transcends language barriers and cultural differences.

And the way they frame the shot? Utterly endearing. As they count down—three, two, one (San, Ni, Ichi) —their enthusiasm is contagious, and the shutter clicks, freezing our joy in pixels.

What strikes me most is their unwavering respect—for their own people and for us, the foreigners. It's a lesson in kindness, a reminder that compassion knows no boundaries.

These lovely Japanese souls teach us that sometimes, the most beautiful memories are made not through our own lenses, but through the lens of shared humanity.

My encounter with a doctor was unforgettable, and not in the way you'd expect! One day, I suddenly developed a skin infection on my face. Naturally, I turned to Google to find a nearby dermatologist. As soon as I entered the clinic, I was stopped at the reception and handed an application form—in Japanese, of course. Thank goodness for Google Translate!

Next, the receptionist asked if I had a face mask. I sheepishly admitted I didn't (even during COVID, I wasn't a fan of masks). She promptly pulled one out and said, "100 Yen." Without a word, I handed over the cash. Then came the insurance card request. Alas, I had forgotten it at home. I assured her I'd pay out of pocket, and she directed me to the waiting area.

After a 30-minute wait, I was finally called into the doctor's cabin. Inside was a middle-aged lady doctor who didn't speak a word of English. Remember, this was my first visit to a doctor in two years! I resorted to typing my symptoms on my phone, and she responded using a microphone. Within two minutes, she understood my problem and offered a solution. Apparently, skin allergies are common in Japan during winter.

She then took out an ointment tube and demonstrated how to apply it. I was amazed at her meticulousness. Later, I went to the pharmacy with my prescription. The pharmacist handed me yet another form to fill out (thank you, Google Translate, once again). She then explained, in Japanese, how to use the ointment. I nodded along, trying to keep up.

As I left the pharmacy, I couldn't help but shout, "God, please keep me healthy! I don't want to visit any more doctors in Japan!" Jokes aside, the medical system here is absolutely top-notch, albeit expensive. It's no wonder the Japanese have such long lifespans!

We booked a Kyoto tour with "Get Your Guide," a top-notch tour operator in Japan. Our itinerary included three famous temples and the enchanting Arashiyama bamboo grove.

At the crack of dawn, precisely 8 AM, we hopped on the bus. Our guide was a charming elderly lady who spoke English, Chinese, and Japanese fluently. (Pro tip: Always check if your tour has an English-speaking guide before booking!)

After exploring the first temple, we were instructed to be back by 12 Noon sharp to head to the next destination. We returned at 12:02 PM, and our guide immediately started grumbling about our tardiness. I tried to reason with her, saying it was just 2 minutes, but she was having none of it.

Despite the fuss, the bus didn't budge. Turns out, another couple was missing. I glanced at the guide and asked what she planned to do. With a cool demeanor, she instructed the driver to start the bus.

I was flabbergasted! As the bus began to move, I spotted the missing couple sprinting towards us. I yelled, "Look, they're coming!" They apologized profusely, explaining they couldn't remember which bus was ours amidst the sea of parked buses.

From that moment on, I made sure we were always 5 minutes early. At the end of the trip, the guide came over and apologized for the earlier incident.

The moral of the story? Japanese people treat time like gold. Their punctuality isn't just a professional trait; it's a way of life.

Unforgettable Shikoku Trip

We embarked on a New Year adventure to Shikoku, blending pilgrimage with pleasure. This spiritual journey was a treat, thanks to the locals who pampered us pilgrims like royalty.

Words fail to capture the beauty of Shikoku islands —it's simply breathtaking. Picture mountains, forests, rivers, and lush agricultural lands. It was a tour to remember!

Our journey began at the first temple in Tokushima, and we managed to cover four temples on foot. And by "walking," I mean hiking up hills that made us question our life choices. We donned the full pilgrimage attire: a white robe (hakue/oizuru), a sedge hat (sugegasa), and a walking stick (kongōzue). We looked like we were auditioning for a historical drama!

On the third day, New Year's Eve, we were strolling down the road in our pilgrimage gear when a middle-aged lady suddenly burst out of her shop and stopped us. Shocked, I had no idea what was happening. By now, I could understand a bit of Japanese.

She asked where we were from. I replied, "INDIA." Her face lit up like a Christmas tree. "INDIA… wow, the home of Buddha!" she exclaimed. I nodded, and she invited us into her shop.

We went inside, took a seat, and she vanished into the depths of her shop. We waited for five minutes, clueless about what to do next. She reappeared with two cups of hot green tea and some biscuits. We were astonished by her kindness.

She told us we were the first Indians she'd met this season. I felt so happy and, with my broken Japanese, said we loved exploring Japan. Then she asked if we followed Buddhism. I explained that we were Hindus.

After 15 minutes, we decided to leave, and she disappeared again. She returned with a plastic bag filled with fruits and biscuits and offered them to us. We were stunned by her generosity and thanked her profusely.

This experience showed us the incredible kindness of the Japanese people. Later, I learned that these offerings are a tradition in the Shikoku pilgrimage, known as 'osettai' (お接待), where locals provide food, snacks, and water to pilgrims.

A Remarkable Encounter with Japan's Lost & Found System

During a recent visit to the Landmark Tower in Yokohama, Japan, I stopped by an ATM to withdraw some cash. Everything seemed routine—until I reached the subway station and realized something was missing: one of my Air Pods.

It was late, and although I was fairly certain I had lost it somewhere within the Landmark Tower, I decided to head home and return the next day.

After work, I made my way back to Landmark Tower and approached the information desk. I explained to the staff that I had lost an Air Pod the previous day. The attendant, a kind and smiling lady, asked me to wait while she made a phone call. After a brief moment, she turned to me and said, “Please proceed to the Lost & Found counter.”

Curious and hopeful, I asked, “Has it been found?” She smiled again and simply replied, “Yes.”

I hurried to the Lost & Found counter, where I was greeted by yet another friendly staff member. Upon seeing me, she immediately reached beneath the desk and produced a small plastic pouch. Inside was my missing Air Pod.

I was genuinely astonished. In a bustling public space, someone had found my Air Pod, turned it in, and the system had preserved it safely until I returned. I need to fill in a form at the counter and received it in good condition.

This experience was a testament to the integrity, efficiency, and thoughtfulness embedded in Japanese society. The fact that a small item like an Air Pod could be recovered so seamlessly speaks volumes.

Our movie adventures

Rajni has a massive fan following in Japan, and believe it or not, there's even a fan club for him here!

As a die-hard Rajnikant fan, I was thrilled when Thalaivar's movie "Jailor" was released in Japan. With great excitement, we headed to the theater for the First Day First Show (FDFS), reminiscing about our lively experiences back home.

But to our surprise, the theater was as calm as a library! We were instructed not to make any noise during the movie... which is a far cry from the energetic atmosphere in Chennai.

When Thalaivar made his grand entrance, there were no whistles, no claps, nothing. Just absolute silence. You could hear a pin drop, except for the movie's audio.

I turned to my friend and whispered, "Are we in a movie theater or a meditation retreat?"

Feeling a bit let down, we decided to avoid watching movies in Japan from then on.

Fast forward to the release of "Mission Impossible – The Last Reckoning" in IMAX. Being a huge 'Tom Cruise fan', I couldn't resist giving it another shot.

Hoping for a different experience this time, I entered the IMAX theater. But oh boy, it was déjà vu! Pin drop silence again... and everyone stayed seated until the very last credit rolled.

I leaned over and joked, "I think Tom Cruise would be more shocked by this silence than by any of his stunts!"

This time, I made up my mind: no more movies in Japan for me!

CHAPTER 7

UNIQUE THINGS YOU WILL FIND ONLY IN JAPAN

Japan boasts numerous unique customs and traditions that often evoke a sense of astonishment. Let's explore some of these fascinating aspects of Japanese culture:

Bowing of Respect:

In Japan, bowing is a common form of greeting. People frequently bow to convey respect and gratitude to others. The depth and duration of the bow can vary based on the context and relationship.

For those experiencing this cultural practice for the first time, it can be a surprising gesture with various meanings.

Shoes On and Off:

A customary practice in Japan is removing shoes before entering a home. Indoors, people go barefoot or wear indoor slippers.

For foreigners accustomed to wearing shoes indoors, this can be a fresh and unusual experience. It reflects cleanliness and respect for the living space.

New Year's Monetary Gifts:

Japan has a tradition of giving monetary gifts called "Otoshidama" to children during the New Year. Children eagerly anticipate these gifts, while adults prepare "Pochi Bukuro" envelopes with bills to give when visiting relatives' homes.

This unique practice might raise eyebrows but is deeply rooted in Japanese culture and customs.

Queuing Culture:

Japan values orderly queues in various settings, such as waiting for public transportation or at popular shops and attractions.

Many people don't hesitate to join long lines, and the efficiency and orderliness of this habit can be astonishing to outsiders.

Tea Culture:

Tea holds significant importance in Japan, with a unique ceremony known as "Sadou" or tea ceremony.

The preparation and etiquette surrounding tea, such as how it's brewed and consumed, are governed by formal rules. Engaging with these rituals can be a deeply intriguing experience.

Chopstick Etiquette:

While dining in Japan involves the use of chopsticks, there are intricate manners regarding their use and handling.

Observing Japanese people skillfully maneuver chopsticks can be a novel sight for visitors.

Pachinko Culture:

Pachinko, a form of gambling, is part of Japan's gaming culture enjoyed by many.

The way pachinko is played uniquely in Japan might pique your curiosity. It involves vertical pinball-like machines and is a blend of skill and chance.

Train Crowds:

In urban areas of Japan, trains can become extremely crowded during rush hours and events like fireworks festivals.

Encountering packed trains and the hustle and bustle of commuters might be a novel experience for travelers.

Station Melodies:

Japanese train stations play distinctive melodies to signal train arrivals and departures.

Experiencing different melodies at various stations can be an amusing adventure for anyone traveling by train in Japan.

Politeness in Service:

Japanese service industries prioritize polite customer service, making interactions with waitstaff, shopkeepers, and service providers exceptionally courteous and respectful.

These customs are not only unique but also integral to the fabric of Japanese society. They reflect the nation's rich history, cultural values, and the art of harmonizing tradition with modernity

When I started thinking about unique things in Japan, first thing which came to my mind is the TOILET. Yes, don't be surprised, as I have not seen such advanced toilets in my life.

Unveiling Japan's Magical Toilets: Where Hygiene Meets Hi-Tech!

Ah, behold the humble restroom—a gateway to relief, contemplation, and dare I say, "enlightenment."

Comfort and Cleanliness of Japanese toilets

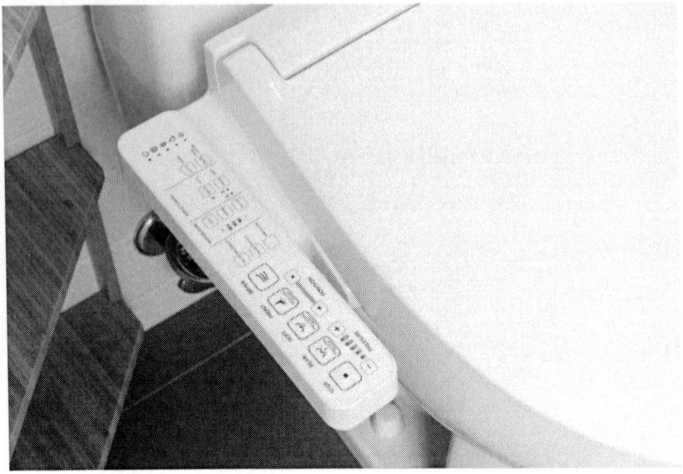

1. The Bidet Ballet: A Rear-Washing Extravaganza
   Picture this: You perch upon the throne, ready for business. But wait! A secret awaits beneath the seat—a bidet nozzle. Yes, my friend, it's showtime! With the grace of a ballerina, the bidet pirouettes into action, spraying your posterior with a gentle stream of water. It's like a spa day for your derrière.
   And guess what? Some models even have an extra wand for the ladies. Because equality, my friends—equality even in the loo!
2. Toasty Tushies: The Heated Seat Symphony
   Winter mornings in Japan can be frostier than a snowman's handshake. Fear not! The heated toilet seat

cradles your behind like a warm hug from a friendly robot. It's like sitting on a cloud infused with cozy vibes.

But wait, there's more! These seats are smarter than your average bear. They know when you're coming, like mystical seat-whisperers. So, during warmer months, they politely switch off to save energy. Talk about seat-sational efficiency!

3. Air Ballet for Your Booty: The Drying Overture

   You've been bidet-blessed, and now your nether regions glisten like dew-kissed petals. But what's this? A gentle breeze caresses your dampness away. Yes, my friend, it's the toilet dryer—a symphony of air currents that leaves your posterior as pristine as a freshly laundered kimono.

   And the best part? You're saving trees! No more wasteful paper—just a breezy farewell to moisture.

4. The Regal Flap Waltz: Automatic Lid Etiquette

   As you approach the porcelain throne, the lid rises—majestic and welcoming. It's like the toilet saying, "Ah, honored guest, step forth!"

   And when you're done, a gentle tilt, and the lid descends—a polite curtain call. We've witnessed Shakespearean dramas less elegant than this. Bravo, Japanese toilets, bravo!

5. Water Temperature Tango and Pressure Polka
   Fancy a hot-water cleanse? Most models let you adjust the temperature. It's like Goldilocks finding her "just right."
   And the water pressure? Oh, it's customizable too! Front wash, back wash—choose your dance partner. These toilets are like your personal hygienic DJs, spinning the perfect track for your tush.
6. Cleanliness Chronicles: The Saga of Spotless Thrones
   Public restrooms? Fear not! Japanese toilets are like cleanliness ninjas. They're always clean and dry, even in bustling train stations or serene temples. It's like they've taken a vow of perpetual purity.
   So, roam freely, fellow wanderer. Whether you're at a shrine, a ramen joint, or a cat café (yes, even cat cafés have posh potties), relief awaits.
   When you flush the toilet, the water gets filled through an open tap, and you know this is for washing your hands. That is awesome, isn't it?
   And there you have it—the saga of Japan's toilets, where technology meets tact, and every flush is a standing ovation. So next time you visit, bow to the porcelain gods—they've got your back(side).

Collection of stamps at Shrines (Goshuin) on railway stations (Eki) World heritage sites and important sites, and finally the food outlets are another unique thing I noticed in Japan.

"Goshuin: Stamps of Devotion and Aesthetic Splendor"

Dating back nearly 1300 years, the ancient practice of goshuin finds its roots in unwavering faith. Imagine pilgrims, their hearts aflame with devotion, meticulously handwriting Buddhist sutras—shakyo—and dedicating them to revered temples. In return, they received a goshuin, a sacred seal bestowed by the temple's nuns and monks.

Fast-forward to modern times, where the practice has evolved. No longer confined to sutra transcription, visitors can now acquire a goshuin through a different ritual. By paying a nominal fee (usually ranging from ¥300 to ¥1000) or making a donation, they receive this treasured stamp. And it's not just pilgrims anymore; a new generation has embraced goshuin collection as a delightful hobby. These enthusiasts flaunt their unique finds on social media—adorable, seasonal, or remarkably aesthetic goshuin from lesser-known temples and shrines.

The goshuincho, a sacred ledger, plays a pivotal role. Its pages bear witness to pilgrimages, each stamp a testament to faith. These books, still in use today, serve as tangible records. Yet, perhaps, their spiritual weight has lightened over time.

Now, let's embark on a goshuin adventure! Picture yourself stepping into a temple or shrine. Seek out the reception area, where keychains and omamori beckon. Look for signs in elegant kanji: Goshuinjo, Shuinjo, or Noukyoujo at temples, and Goshuinjo, Juyojo, or Shamusho at shrines.

Hand over your goshuincho (a small notebook) and pay the fee. Some shrines offer multiple goshuin options—choose one or collect them all. But remember, during this sacred exchange, no photos or videos allowed.

As for me, I've amassed over 50 goshuin this year—a cherished trove of memories.

A picture of Goshuin stamp

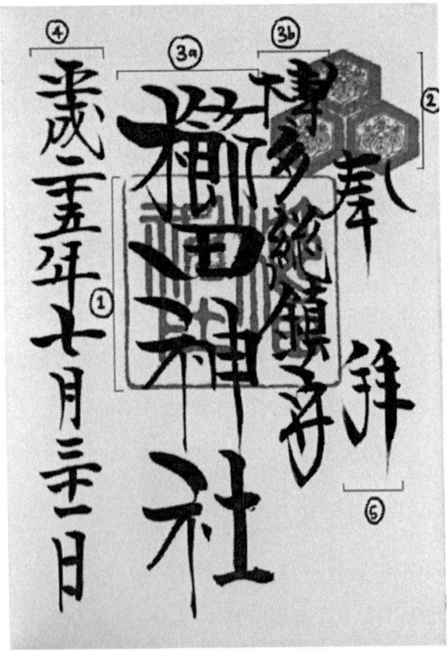

Decoding Your First Goshuin: A Visual Journey

The Grand Red Stamp

At the heart of each goshuin lies the shrine or temple's name. In our example, the kanji '櫛田神社' graces the page, signifying Kushida-jinja.

Petite Red Symbols

These smaller red stamps represent the deities honored by the shrine or temple. In Fukuoka's Kushida-jinja, three hexagons symbolize Hakata's patron Gods: Amaterasu Omikami, Ohatanushi no Omikami, and Susano no Omikami.

Central Calligraphy

a. Largest Calligraphy: The shrine or temple's name—'櫛田神社'—in bold Kanji.

b. Smaller Calligraphy: Sometimes, names exceed a few characters. Here, '博多総鎮守' (Hakata Souchinju) accompanies the main name, elegantly flanking it.

Left-Side Date

The Kanji here marks your visit's date: 平成二十五年、七月、三十一日—July 31st, 2013, in the 25th year of the Heisei era.

Right-Side Reverence

Words like '崇拝,' '奉拝,' '参拝', or '遥拝'—all evoke worship, adoration, and reverence.

Eki Stamps: Unveiling Japan's Railway Quest

Imagine crisscrossing Japan with your trusty Japan Rail Pass, not merely to traverse landscapes, but to unravel a unique tradition: collecting Eki train stamps. These aren't your run-of-the-mill ink imprints; they're miniature masterpieces, each station boasting its own artistic flair. Let's dive into this enchanting pastime!

What Are Eki Stamps?

Eki stamps, lovingly nestled within train stations, are more than ink on paper. They're snapshots of local character—tiny canvases that whisper tales of the locale.

Picture this: Fukui in 1931, where the first eki stamp made its debut. Its mission? To ignite local tourism, especially among the young. And oh, how it spread! Now, over 9,000 train stations across Japan bear these inked signatures.

But wait, there's more! Some stations unveil limited editions and seasonal stamps, like secret treasures waiting to be discovered.

How to Collect Eki Stamps?

The Stamp Stations Await: Wander through train stations, eyes wide like a curious cat. There, near ticket gates, station master's offices, or cozy waiting areas, you'll find stamp stations. They beckon, inkpads at the ready.

Your Passport to Adventure: Whip out your eki stamp book—about the size of a passport, thick pages guarding against ink seepage. Press it onto the inked pad, and voilà! A memento blooms—a tiny piece of station magic.

Friendly Station Staff: Lost? Fear not! The friendly station staff will guide you. They're like navigational wizards, pointing you to the nearest stamp oasis.

Mountain-Top Stamps: Even Owakudani ropeway station in Hakone boasts its own stamp. Imagine collecting one at the summit, clouds swirling around you. It's like capturing a piece of sky.

Eki Stamp Book Sizes and Styles

Eki stamp books come in various sizes, but the classic one is passport-sized, with around 50 pages. These pages are sturdy, guarding against ink smudges.

Feeling rebellious? Grab any notebook or surface you fancy. Eki counters often stash loose papers for stamping—because creativity knows no bounds.

Do All Stations Have Stamps?

Yes, indeed! From bustling city hubs to sleepy rural stops, most train stations in Japan flaunt their unique eki stamps. Even Tokyo Station joins the party, its inked secrets waiting to be unlocked.

(Subway do not have stamps)

Additionally, stamps are available at major tourist attractions.

Locker system

Japan offers a highly convenient locker system at train stations and airports, making it easy for travelers to store their luggage securely while exploring.

Train Stations

1. Types of Lockers:

– Key-operated lockers: Simple to use; insert coins, lock the door, and keep the key.

– Keyless lockers: Operated via touch panels; payment can be made using cash or IC cards like Suica or PASMO.
– Smartphone-enabled lockers: Available in major stations; allow remote availability checks, advance reservations, and cashless payments.

2. Sizes and Costs:
– Small: Suitable for bags and backpacks; costs around 300-400 yen.
– Medium: Fits carry-on bags; costs around 500-600 yen.
– Large: Suitable for standard suitcases; costs around 700-800 yen.
– Extra-Large: Limited availability; costs around 900 yen

3. Usage Tips:
– Lockers can be rented for up to three days.
– Availability may vary, especially during peak travel seasons
– Instructions are often available in multiple languages

Airports

1. Availability:
– Major airports like Narita and Haneda offer locker services.
– Lockers are typically located near baggage claim areas and in various terminals.

2. Types and Costs:
- Similar to train stations, airports offer a range of locker sizes to accommodate different luggage types.
- Costs are comparable to those at train stations, with fees ranging from 300 to 800 yen depending on size and duration.

3. Additional Services:
- Some airports provide luggage storage counters for larger items or longer storage durations.
- These counters may offer additional services like luggage wrapping and delivery'

Using these lockers can significantly enhance your travel experience by allowing you to explore without the burden of heavy bags.

Natural hot springs of Japan – another unique wonder

"Onsen: Where Tradition Meets Wellness"

Improves Blood Circulation

Picture this: You slip into the warm embrace of an onsen, and as the steam envelops you, your blood vessels dilate. The heat works its magic, enhancing circulation. Those arteries? They relax and expand, ushering in a sense of calm. It's like a gentle massage for your insides.

Relieves Pain and Sore Muscles

Your tired body finds solace in the onsen's mineral-rich waters. Tight muscles? They surrender to the warmth. Inflammation? It retreats, defeated. As you soak, the pain eases, and you emerge feeling lighter—like a well-kneaded loaf of bread.

Reduces Stress

The onsen whispers secrets to your soul. Its soothing waters cradle you, washing away worries. Stress? It dissolves, leaving behind tranquility. Close your eyes, breathe in the steam, and let your mind float—a mental spa day, courtesy of nature.

Better Sleep

Imagine slipping into an onsen just before bedtime. The water cradles you, lulling your mind into serenity. Your body unwinds, tension slipping away. When you finally crawl under the covers, sleep embraces you like a soft kimono. Sweet dreams, weary traveler.

Restores and Cures

Onsen minerals weave their magic. They kiss your skin, soothing and healing. Softness blooms, like cherry blossoms in spring. And deep within, your wellness stirs—a symphony of rejuvenation. It's not just water; it's liquid restoration.

Boosts Metabolism

Regular onsen baths? They're like a turbocharger for your body's engine. Metabolism revs up, cells humming with newfound energy. As you soak, you're not just cleansing; you're igniting vitality.

Rules for Onsen:

Generally, there are separate onsen bath for males and females.

One need to be fully undressed for onsen.

Preparing for the Onsen Experience

Before heading to a bathhouse, pack a few essentials:

Towel: While most establishments provide towels, bringing your own ensures you're comfortable. Especially, a small towel is necessary when you take a public bath.

Soap and shampoo: Some bathhouses may not supply these, although many sell ones. Especially if you have your favorite soap, shampoo, or rinse, bring some to use as usual.

Before getting into the onsen bath, one need to take a complete bath. The facilities are available nearby the bath area.

The hot water temperature will be around 42-45 degree Celsius. Hence first put your feet down, then slowly up to hip level, and once you feel comfortable immerse yourself fully. Some people put a wet towel on head to balance the temperature.

Don't spend more than ten minutes at a time. come out relax and again get in.

There are onsen shower area inside as well as sauna at few places.

Once done, again take a bath before leaving the area. (some theory says, don't use soap, because the herbs may be wiped out)

Relax for 30 minutes before getting into any other activity.

Drink plenty of water before and after onsen.

I will tell you onsen is awesome experience.

Etiquette is Key

When at an onsen or sento (Artificial Onsen), it's crucial to respect the local customs:

Clean First: Before entering the communal bath, clean your body. This is a sign of respect, ensuring the water remains clean for everyone.

No Swimwear: While some places allow visitors to wear swimwear, it's more usual to take such public baths in the nude (only with a small towel).

Keep Quiet: Conversations should be kept low. The bathhouse is a place of relaxation and contemplation.

Tie Up Long Hair: If you have long hair, tie it up to prevent it from touching the water.

Don't soak your towel in the water: This is also in order to keep the water clean. You can put the towel on your head, perhaps.

Don't color your hair: Believe or not, somebody does this in the public bath, and some places has a notice to warn their visitors against it. Of course, you should not, because it is not your own bathroom.

Too much of tattoos on body is sometimes not allowed.

Difference between onsen and sento

Before diving in, it's essential to understand the difference between onsen and sento. While both are public baths, an onsen is a naturally occurring hot spring rich in minerals, believed to have healing properties. A sento, on the other hand, is a man-made public bathhouse, often found in urban areas.

Manholes on the footpath and on the roads:

Why Tourists Should Look To The Ground While Walking Around In A Japanese City

Leave it to Japan and its detail-oriented culture to transform something associated with the lowest and dirtiest of places into a work of high art. In this country, even the design of manhole covers has become a thriving art form, one that inspires "drain spotters" or "manholers" to go searching for special sewer entrances on city streets. While you're sightseeing here, remember to check the ground, as you may be stepping right over one of these decorative manhole (aka maintenance hole) covers. They're almost the perfect bookend to a sanitation process that begins with high-tech toilets.

Keep your eyes peeled for designer maintenance covers

The beautification of Japanese maintenance covers reportedly began in the 1970s and 1980s as cities sought support for tax-funded sanitation improvements. Today, many cities have maintenance covers scattered about with depictions of local landmarks or mascots. Not every cover boasts a colorful pattern; some may be plain cast iron or without any design. However, in Osaka, which has twice hosted the world expo, you could stumble across one showing the mascot for Expo 2025, for instance.

Off-season, in the sumo neighborhood of Ryogoku, Tokyo, you might be surprised to see a maintenance cover reproducing the ukiyo-e artist Hokusai's famous print, "The Great Wave," aka "Under the Wave off Kanagawa." The Sumida Hokusai Museum is nearby, hence the use of a sewer lid as the unlikely canvas for such a world-renowned piece of art. Elsewhere in Tokyo, while you're hunting the real-life landmarks demolished by Godzilla onscreen, you can find the King of Monsters depicted on two maintenance covers outside the Shinjuku Toho Building.

Collect maintenance hole cover cards or photos

Forget the augmented reality of Pokémon Go. If you really want to interact with your surroundings — and take your drain spotting to the next level — try actively seeking out Japan's designer maintenance covers with maps on sites like Poké Lids. It shows where all the Pokémon-themed covers are in different cities around the country.

The art of maintenance covers has become so popular in Japan that it's even inspired a collectible card series. An organization called GKP, which stands for Gesui Koho Purattohomu ("Sewer System PR Platform"), distributes the cards to drain spotters through local sewerage and tourist information centers. That's right: the sewer has a public relations team here.

Even if you're not into the cards, you can always start your own collection of maintenance cover photos. This follows the spirit of Japanese stamp rallies, where people go around collecting stamps as they travel to different places. When you're walking around Kobe, and you suddenly find yourself looking down at a maintenance cover with the city's name and skyline on it, it might feel silly to stop and point your camera down at the sewer. Yet even a casual bit of drain spotting could take you off the beaten path for a moment and show the care that went into decorating an everyday sewer lid with street art.

Hanami (Admiring Flowers):

Hanami is the tradition of viewing flowers, particularly sakura (cherry blossoms). People gather under these delicate pink blooms during springtime to appreciate their beauty.

It's a centuries-old custom that originated during the Nara era (710-794) and was initially reserved for the nobility. Today, it's one of the most beloved springtime activities in Japan.

Whether in quiet gardens or bustling parks, hanami brings people together to celebrate the fleeting beauty of cherry blossoms.

Kintsugi (Golden Repair):

Kintsugi is the art of repairing broken pottery using gold or silver lacquer. Instead of hiding imperfections, this technique highlights them, turning flaws into beautiful designs.

It's a metaphor for the wabi-sabi philosophy, which appreciates the beauty of imperfection and impermanence.

Kintsugi celebrates the idea that even broken things can be made whole again, more beautiful for having been broken.

Ikebana (Way of Flowers):

Ikebana, also known as kad, is the Japanese art of flower arranging. It's not just about aesthetics; it's a form of expression.

Ikebana follows specific rules, including considerations of material choice and arranging form based on concepts of good and evil fortune.

Various schools of thought, such as Ikenobo, Sogetsu, and Ohara, practice ikebana. It's both a creative outlet and a form of meditation.

Senninbari (Thousand-Stitch Belt):

The traditional Japanese belt-making custom known as senninbari involves creating a belt with 1,000 stitches.

Historically, women made these belts for soldiers going off to war, believing that the stitches would protect them from harm.

Each stitch symbolized a prayer for the soldier's safety, making senninbari a unique and heartfelt tradition.

These customs reflect Japan's history, culture, and temperament, making them captivate to explore. Whether it's celebrating cherry blossoms, embracing imperfections, arranging flowers, or stitching protective belts, Japan's uniqueness shines through its cherished traditions.

Calligraphy:

Japanese calligraphy, known as shodō (書道), is a revered art form that combines aesthetics, tradition, and expression. Originating from Chinese calligraphy, it evolved to include unique Japanese styles with the introduction of hiragana and katakana.

Shodō emphasizes the beauty of each brushstroke, creating elegant and meaningful characters. It's not just about writing; it's about capturing the spirit and emotion behind the words.

Shinkansen:

On October 1, 1964, the first Shinkansen line, known as the 'Tokaido Shinkansen', commenced commercial service between Tokyo and Osaka.

This groundbreaking event coincided with the Tokyo Olympics, marking a new era in rail travel

Certain things cannot be explained by words, it should be experienced. This applies to Shinkansen. Wow, it is a marvel.

1. The Shin-sational Stations:
   The shinkansen stations are like the VIP lounges of the railway world. They don't just have names; they have titles. Imagine if your local subway station had a prefix like "Supreme" or "Galactic." Well, the shinkansen stations are all about that life. Yokohama? Nah, it's "Shin Yokohama." Tokyo? Pfft, try "Shin Tokyo." It's like they're saying, "Regular stations, step aside. The shin is in town!"
2. The D-Day Drama:
   We arrived at the station an hour early because, let's face it, shinkansen time is different. It's like Narnia—you step inside, and suddenly, hours morph into minutes. As the clock ticked down, the platform trembled. Was it an earthquake? Nope. It was the shinkansen, flexing its muscles. The first look? Mind-blowing. It

was sleeker than a dolphin in a tuxedo, shinier than a freshly polished samurai sword. Real beauty, my friends.

3. The Need for Speed:
   Boarding the shinkansen felt like stepping into an aircraft on rails. The doors slid shut, and we were off. The acceleration? Hold onto your sushi rolls, folks. We hit 300-310 kmph faster than you can say "wasabi." The scenery outside? A blur. Trees bowed down in respect, birds gave us high-fives (or wing-fives, rather), and clouds whispered, "You're doing great, sweetie."
   And the best part? The tray tables. Oh, those magical trays! You could place a cup of coffee on them, do a somersault, and the coffee wouldn't spill. It's like they hired wizards to design those trays. "Accio, spill-proof!" they chanted.
4. Spacious and Wi-Fi-fied:
   Inside, it was roomier than a penthouse suite. Legroom? More than enough to stretch out and practice your ninja kicks. Wi-Fi? Faster than a ninja's reflexes. Toilets? Neat, pristine, and probably cleaned by ninja janitors. I half-expected a tiny voice to say, "Welcome to the Shinkansen Spa. Please enjoy your refreshing bathroom experience."
5. Hiroshima Express:
   Less than four hours later (800 kilometers—who's counting?), we arrived in Hiroshima. The shinkansen

had sliced through space-time like a katana through tofu. We stepped out, wobbly-legged, but with hearts full of awe. Hiroshima greeted us with open arms, and I swear I heard it whisper, "You've just ridden the shin-tastic express. You're officially cooler than a snowman in shades."

And so, my friends, that's how my first shinkansen adventure unfolded—a tale of speed, elegance, and coffee-friendly trays. If you ever find yourself aboard the bullet train, remember: You're not just traveling; you're transcending.

Tea ceremonies **(Chanoyu)**

Step into a tatami-matted room, where time slows like a koi fish in a pond. The tea ceremony, or chanoyu, isn't just about matcha and delicate cups—it's a meditation. Each movement—the whisk, the bowl, the silence—is deliberate. It's like coding in C++: precise, elegant, and Zen. And guess what? The antioxidants in green tea are like debugging tools for your cells. They fix glitches and keep your code (read: body) running smoothly

Haiku

A haiku is a traditional Japanese form of poetry consisting of three lines with a syllable pattern of 5-7-5. Haikus often capture moments in nature or seasonal changes, using simple yet evocative language to convey deep emotions and observations.

They typically include a “kigo” (seasonal word) and a “kireji” (cutting word) to create a pause or juxtaposition.

You can find few haiku poems in this book.

Anime

Anime and Animation

Anime and animation hold a significant place in Japanese culture, appealing to a wide audience through various forms such as books, movies, games, and more. Here’s why they’re so popular:

Diverse Content: Anime spans a wide range of genres, from action and romance to science fiction and fantasy, ensuring there’s something for everyone.

Artistic Quality: The unique art style of anime, with its vibrant colors and expressive characters, is visually appealing and has become iconic worldwide.

Unique Storytelling: Anime often features complex narratives and character development that can be both engaging and emotionally resonant.

Cultural Appeal: Anime incorporates elements of Japanese culture, which can be both educational and fascinating for international audiences.

Historical Roots: The tradition of storytelling through art is deeply rooted in Japanese history, with modern anime drawing on these cultural practices.

Global Phenomenon: The popularity of anime has crossed borders, becoming a global phenomenon with a dedicated fanbase.

Technological Advancements: The rise of streaming services and gaming has made anime more accessible than ever, contributing to its widespread popularity.

Anime and its related media are not just a form of entertainment but also an influential part of Japan's cultural export, contributing significantly to the country's soft power.

It's a testament to the creativity and innovation of Japanese storytelling and animation techniques

Astroboy, and Akira are some of the famous Anime series in Japan.

Manga

Manga refers to Japanese comic books or graphic novels. It's a written medium that is typically published in black and white, except for the covers and sometimes a few pages inside.

Readers engage with manga by reading from right to left, which is the traditional Japanese reading direction.

Manga series can be expansive, often serialized in magazines before being compiled into volumes

The main difference lies in the consumption method: manga is read, while anime is watched

Board games

In Japan, both traditional and modern board games are popular. Here are some of the most famous ones:

Go (Igo): Originated in China, Go is believed to be one of the most ancient board games in the world. The game involves capturing as many stones of your opponent as possible.

Shogi: Often compared to chess, Shogi is a strategic board game that is widely played in Japan.

Gomoku: A simple yet engaging game where the goal is to line up five markers in a row.

Sugoroku: A Japanese board game which has two versions: ban-sugoroku (similar to backgammon) and e-sugoroku (which is similar to snakes and ladders).

Japanese Mahjong: A variation of the classic game Mahjong, it is a game of skill, strategy, and calculation.

Catan: Known worldwide, Catan is also popular in Japan. It's a settlement and road-building game based on a hex and dice rolling system.

Blokus: A colorful, strategic board game that can be played with up to four players.

Battle Line: A two-player, card-based board game inspired by ancient warfare.

Terraforming Mars: A strategy and economy-based game where players work together to terraform Mars.

Tokyo Highway: A modern Japanese board game that is becoming more popular.

These games offer a variety of experiences, from strategic battles to peaceful city-building, catering to different tastes and preferences.

Origami:

Origami is the traditional Japanese art of paper folding, transforming a simple sheet of paper into intricate designs and figures.

The word "origami" comes from the Japanese words "oru" (to fold) and "kami" (paper)

This craft ranges from simple models like cranes and flowers to complex structures like dragons and modular shapes. Origami not only fosters creativity and patience but also serves as a relaxing and meditative activity.

Ikigai

Ikigai is a concept that means "reason for being." It involves finding a balance between what you love, what you are good at, what the world needs, and what you can be paid for. For example, a chef who loves cooking, excels at it, provides delicious meals that people need, and earns a living from it has found their ikigai.

Wabi Sabi

Wabi Sabi is the appreciation of beauty in imperfection and transience. It encourages acceptance of the natural cycle of growth and decay. An example is a cracked ceramic bowl that gains character and beauty over time.

Ganbatte

Ganbatte means "do your best" or "keep going." It's often used to encourage someone facing a challenge. For instance, a student might say "Ganbatte!" to a friend before an exam.

5S

5S is a workplace organization method that stands for Seiri (Sort), Seiton (Set in Order), Seiso (Shine), Seiketsu

(Standardize), and Shitsuke (Sustain). It aims to improve efficiency and safety. For example, in a factory, tools are sorted, organized, cleaned, standardized, and maintained regularly.

Kaizen

Kaizen means "continuous improvement." It involves making small, incremental changes to improve processes. An example is a company that regularly holds meetings to discuss and implement small improvements in their workflow.

Kanban

Kanban is a scheduling system for lean manufacturing and just-in-time production. It uses visual signals to indicate when new supplies are needed. For example, a factory might use cards to signal when a part needs to be replenished.

Hara Hachi Bu

Hara Hachi Bu is a practice of eating until you are 80% full. It promotes mindful eating and longevity. Okinawans, known for their long lifespans, follow this practice to maintain health.

Shikata ga nai

Shikata ga nai means "it cannot be helped" or "nothing can be done about it." It reflects acceptance of situations beyond one's control. For example, during natural disasters, people might use this phrase to express resilience.

Shoshin

Shoshin means "beginner's mind." It encourages openness and eagerness to learn without preconceptions. In martial arts, practitioners maintain shoshin to continuously improve their skills.

"Our Inaugural Zazen Encounter"

As a dedicated practitioner of Yoga and meditation, I have spent over eight years faithfully following Sadguru's Sambhavi Maha Mudra. This daily practice has granted me a measure of control over my body and mind, although enlightenment remains elusive.

Recently, my curiosity led me to explore Zazen—a venerable meditation technique with roots in ancient Japan. Living in Yokohama, I discovered that the SOJIJI (Zen) Temple offered Zazen classes in English on weekends.

One crisp Saturday morning, my journey unfolded. The sprawling Sojiji Temple, dating back to the 12th and 13th centuries, sprawled across acres—an architectural marvel. A monk greeted us and ushered us into a vast hall, the scheduled class time approaching.

At 9:45 AM, we sat alone, wondering if we were the sole participants. But then, like a harmonious chorus, more than twenty seekers arrived promptly at 9:55 AM. Mostly foreigners, they registered for the class, their eyes reflecting anticipation.

The monk guided us to the meditation hall, where we embarked on an hour of Zazen. Words fail to capture the experience: a silent communion with existence, a dance of stillness. It was, quite simply, awe-inspiring.

Post-Zazen, the monk graciously shared the temple's history. Curious, I asked about his daily routine. His laughter echoed through the hallowed halls as he explained that Zen Buddhism allowed its priests to lead normal family lives. They could eat, drink, and even marry. Assigned to manage specific temples, they balanced sacred duty with earthly bonds.

In the past, monasteries teemed with young acolytes. Now, double-digit attendance was rare. Times change, traditions evolve.

And so, I returned home, dedicating 20 to 40 minutes each evening to Zazen—a quiet voyage within.

Our Tai Chi Adventure

Ever wondered how the Japanese stay so spry even after hitting 70? We stumbled upon some answers in the chapter "Why Japanese Live Longer." One key factor is their daily physical exercise routine (besides Rajio Taizo, of course).

One fine evening, while I was taking a leisurely stroll in the park, I spotted an elderly gentleman, probably around 80, performing some intriguing exercises. It looked like a graceful dance mixed with martial arts moves. Curiosity piqued, I patiently waited for him to finish and approached him to ask what he was doing.

With a smile, he replied, "Tai Chi."

I had heard of Tai Chi ages ago but never paid much attention to it. The next day, I did some Googling and found a Tai Chi school near Yokohama. On a bright Saturday morning, my wife and I decided to visit the school and meet the teacher.

The teacher, who seemed to be in his early 70s but was impressively fit, greeted us warmly. We expressed our interest in joining the weekend class. He informed us that the classes were conducted only in Japanese. Undeterred, we assured him we could manage.

The following week, we joined the class, likely the first Indians to do so. Our batch consisted of 16 students, mostly Japanese, with a few Chinese participants.

Tai Chi, an ancient Chinese martial art, combines gentle, flowing movements with deep breathing and meditation. Often described as "meditation in motion," Tai Chi aims to balance the body's energy (qi) and improve mental and physical health. It involves a series of deliberate postures and movements that promote relaxation, flexibility, and balance.

The literal meaning of Tai Chi, also written as Taijiquan (太極拳), is "supreme ultimate fist" or "boundless fist". "Tai" (太) translates to supreme or ultimate, "Ji" (極) to ultimate or boundary, and "Quan" (拳) to fist or movement. The term emphasizes the martial art's connection to the philosophical concept of the "Great Ultimate," representing the source of all creation and the interplay of yin and yang.

Believe it or not, we started enjoying this art and began practicing regularly. I wholeheartedly recommend Tai Chi to anyone over 50 who wants to stay flexible and fit.

The Heart Sutra in Sanskrit

prajnaparamita hrdaya sutra

om namo bhagavatyai aryaprajnaparamitayai aryavalokitesvaro bodhisattvo gambhiiram prajnaparamitacaryam caramano vyavalokayati sma pancaskandhas tams ca svabhavasunyan pasyati sma

iha sariputra rupam sunyata sunyataiva rupam rupan na prthak sunyata sunyataya na prthag rupam yad rupam sa sunyata ya sunyata tad rupam evam eva vedanasamjnasamskaravijnanam iha sariputra sarvadharmah sunyatalaksana anutpanna aniruddha amala avimala anuna aparipurnah

tasmac chariputra sunyatayam na rupam na vedana na samjna na samskarah na vijnanam na caksuhsrotraghranajihvakayamanamsi na rupasabdagandha rasasprastavyadharmah na caksurdhatur yavan na manovijnanadhatuh navidya navidyaksayo yavan na jaramaranam na jaramaranaksayo na duhkhasamudayanirodhamarga na jnanam na praptir napraptih

tasmac chariputra apraptitvad bodhisattvasya prajnaparamitam asritya viharaty acittavaranah cittavarananastitvad atrasto viparyasatikranto nisthanirvanapraptah tryadhvavyavasthitah

sarvabuddhah prajnaparamitam asrityanuttaram
samyaksambodhim abhisambuddhah

tasmaj jnatavyam prajnaparamita mahamantro
mahavidyamantro nuttaramantro samasamamantrah
sarvaduhkhaprasamanah satyam amithyatvat
prajnaparamitayam ukto mantrah tadyatha

gate gate paragate parasamgate bodhi svaha

iti prajnaparamitahrdayam samaptam

CHAPTER 8

JAPANESE LIVE LONGER

Gentle mountain breeze,
Green tea sips, laughter echoes—
Longevity blooms.

Just across from our apartment lies a 'picturesque park' named "Odori Koen" in Yokohama. Each morning, as I slide open the balcony door, a heartwarming sight awaits me: a group of spirited elderly individuals, most of them in their seventies, diligently engaging in exercises at the precise hour of 6:30 AM.

Come rain or shine, they gather without fail, their unwavering commitment a testament to their resilience. Their chosen exercise routine, known as "Rajio-Taiso," (also called Japanese Gymnastics) has been a cherished tradition in Japan for over a century—an enduring legacy that continues to inspire.

But there's more to this daily spectacle. After their invigorating workout, a select few among them take it upon themselves to tidy up the park. Armed with bags, they diligently collect litter, ensuring that the serene surroundings remain pristine. It's a small yet impactful act of community care—a reflection of the Japanese spirit that values harmony and collective responsibility.

For my wife and me, witnessing this dedicated group has become a source of motivation. Their unwavering commitment to health, camaraderie, and environmental stewardship serves as a reminder that age need not hinder our zest for life. We stand in awe of these remarkable individuals, quietly celebrating their resilience and the beauty they bring to our everyday lives.

Rajio Taiso

("Rajio" means "radio" and "taiso" means "exercise". These Japanese gymnastics, accompanied by classical music (always the same) aims at maintaining good health while improving physical capacities and well-being. It is proven that regular exercise reduces cardiovascular risks and stress.)

When it comes to the life expectancies of people all over the world, Japan comes third in the list of countries. This is quite a feat for the sole nation in the world to have witnessed the devastating power of nuclear weapons.

The average life expectancy of the Japanese people is 82 years, according to the latest United Nations Population Division estimates. One out of 1450 people in Japan is over 100 years old, according to the country's Ministry of Health.

The Japanese are known to be among the fittest and healthiest people in the world.

All this leads us to wonder about the fitness secrets of the Japanese people, who are able to live such long lives. Let us discuss some of the lifestyle choices that set them apart from the others.

High consumption of vegetables

Seafood and meat are a significant part of Japanese cuisine, and so are Japanese veggies. Japan makes extensive use of root vegetables, leafy greens, and other ingredients which are used in soups, desserts, and main courses. Their penchant for vegetables is one of the biggest factors behind their good health.

Physical exercise

The significance of exercise in a nation that is the birthplace of martial arts like Karate, Kendo, Judo and Aikido is self-explanatory. Imperial Japanese used to house well-trained Samurai and the present generation carries the blood of their ancestors, engaging in strong body conditioning and exercise. There are over 1 million people in Japan who have acquired some level of Kendo training as per statistics. So, we can safely assume that physical exercise plays a huge role in their healthy lifestyle.

Method of food preparation

The Japanese have a systematic way of preparing food that is classified into 5 methods.

Nama, which translates to 'raw', describes the way that items are chopped. This is used to prepare delicacies like sashimi that are meant to be eaten raw.

Niru is the precise art of cooking items to the point at which they are perfectly soft and flavorful.

Yaku alludes to the techniques employed to grill food. This entails preparing the ingredients in a small pan with oil or over an open flame, as well as sautéing or shallow frying them.

Musu involves the process of cooking through steam, usually in a pot with a covered lidl bamboo baskets are also used.

Ageru is the practice of deep-frying food at high temperatures while using oil and fat.

Consumption of green tea

The majority of Japanese people include green tea substantially in their daily lives. It is frequently ingested multiple times daily, serving as the preferred beverage first thing in the morning, as well as before and after meals.

High consumption of fish

Japanese include salmon, mackerel, or sardine fish in their diet, which are full of protein and nutrients

Medical facilities

Japan's medical facilities play a significant role in indirectly increasing the life span of its population through various means:

Advanced Medical Technology: Japan is known for its cutting-edge medical technology and equipment, which contribute to early diagnosis and effective treatment of diseases.

Preventive Care: Emphasis on preventive care, including regular health check-ups and screenings, helps in early detection and management of health issues.

Integrated Care Systems: Japan has developed comprehensive care systems that integrate medical care, long-term care, and social welfare services. This holistic approach ensures that elderly individuals receive continuous and coordinated care.

Public Health Initiatives: Government-led public health campaigns promote healthy lifestyles, such as balanced diets, regular exercise, and smoking cessation.

Accessibility and Affordability: Japan's healthcare system is designed to be accessible and affordable for all citizens, reducing barriers to receiving necessary medical care.

Community Support: Community-based support centers provide assistance and resources to elderly individuals, helping them maintain their independence and quality of life.

These factors collectively contribute to Japan's high life expectancy by ensuring that individuals receive timely and effective medical care, maintain healthy lifestyles, and have access to comprehensive support systems.

Japan is renowned for its elderly-friendly and specially-abled-friendly infrastructure. The nation's commitment to inclusivity is evident in the design of its railway stations, shopping malls, airports, and other public facilities, all of which are equipped to accommodate the needs of these two groups. This thoughtful design fosters independence and active participation in daily life for both elderly and specially abled individuals.

In railway stations, special arrangements are made to ensure accessibility for wheelchair users, including ramps, elevators, and designated boarding areas. Additionally, it is a common practice for passengers to offer their seats to elderly individuals upon their entry into the train, reflecting the cultural respect for senior citizens.

Shopping malls and airports are similarly equipped with features such as accessible restrooms, elevators, and clear signage to assist those with mobility challenges. These facilities often include dedicated seating areas and priority lanes to further enhance convenience.

Pets are frequently seen accompanying elderly individuals, and it is common to observe pets being transported in perambulators. This charming sight of pets in prams on the streets adds to the vibrant and inclusive atmosphere of Japanese society.

Overall, Japan's dedication to creating an accessible environment for all its citizens underscores the nation's values of respect, care, and community support.

CHAPTER 9

INSPIRING STORIES

Sakura

Cherry blossoms, heralding the arrival of spring in Japan, are a ubiquitous sight throughout the country. My personal experiences with these beautiful blooms have been particularly memorable at two locations near Tokyo: Ueno Park and Yamataka Jindai Zakura. The latter is home to a remarkable 2,000-year-old Sakura tree, which continues to thrive to this day.

Sakura, or cherry blossoms, offer several profound life lessons:

There is an interesting story, which I came to know, during our visit to Jindai Zakura shrine.

The life cycle of a cherry blossom tree is a beautiful metaphor for the human experience, filled with lessons of impermanence, renewal, and the cyclical nature of life.

Stage 1: Green Buds

As winter draws to a close, the cherry blossom tree begins its transformation. Tiny green buds start to appear on the branches, signaling the end of the cold season. These buds are the first promise of the beauty to come, much like the early stages of human life, filled with potential and promise.

Stage 2: Blossoming Flowers

With the arrival of spring, the buds burst into a spectacular display of pink and white blossoms. This stage, often eagerly anticipated, marks the peak of the tree's beauty. The blossoms typically last for about two weeks, a fleeting period that reminds us of the transient nature of life's most beautiful moments. Just as humans experience the prime of their youth, the cherry blossoms are at their most vibrant and captivating during this time.

Stage 3: Falling Flowers and Growing Leaves

As the blossoms begin to fall, the tree transitions into its next phase. The petals gently drift to the ground, and new leaves start to grow. This stage symbolizes the passage of time and the inevitable changes that come with it. In human life, this can be likened to the transition from youth to maturity, where the initial bloom of youth gives way to the growth of wisdom and experience.

Stage 4: Bare Branches

By summer, the leaves too have fallen, leaving the tree bare once again. This stage represents the later years of life, where the vibrancy of youth has faded, but the essence of life remains. The bare branches stand as a testament to the enduring spirit of the tree, much like the resilience and strength that humans carry into their later years.

The Cycle of Life

Just as the cherry blossom tree goes through its cycle of growth, bloom, and dormancy, humans too experience a similar journey. We grow, blossom, age, and eventually pass on, only to be reborn in new forms, continuing the cycle of life. The impermanence of each stage teaches us to cherish every moment, to find beauty in the transient, and to embrace the constant process of renewal.

Cultural Significance

In Japan, the cherry blossom season is a time of celebration and reflection. The blooming of sakura is welcomed with joy and is considered a symbol of wealth and happiness. Hanami, the tradition of viewing cherry blossoms, brings people together to appreciate the fleeting beauty of the flowers and to celebrate the arrival of spring. This cultural practice underscores the importance of living in the moment and finding joy in the present.

The cherry blossom tree, with its delicate and ephemeral beauty, serves as a poignant reminder of the impermanence of life and the importance of embracing each moment with gratitude and joy.

Bonsai

Bonsai is the ancient Japanese art of cultivating and shaping miniature trees in containers. The term "bonsai" is derived from the Japanese words "bon," meaning tray or container, and "sai," meaning plant or tree.

This practice involves meticulous care, including pruning, wiring, and potting, to create a realistic, miniature representation of nature. Originating over a thousand years ago, bonsai has evolved into a revered art form that combines horticulture and aesthetics, symbolizing harmony, balance, and the beauty of nature in a small, living sculpture.

Growing a bonsai tree at home can be both rewarding and challenging.

Patience and Time: Bonsai cultivation requires significant patience and time. It can take years for a bonsai tree to mature and develop the desired shape

Skill and Techniques: Mastering bonsai techniques such as pruning, wiring, and repotting is essential. These skills are developed over time and through practice

Care and Maintenance: Bonsai trees need constant attention, including regular watering, fertilizing, and monitoring for pests and diseases . The specific care requirements vary depending on the tree species

Environment: Creating the right environment is crucial. Bonsai trees often need specific light, temperature, and humidity conditions to thrive . Indoor bonsai trees, for example, may require grow lights and humidity control .

While it can be challenging, the process of growing a bonsai tree is also deeply fulfilling. With dedication and proper care, you can create a beautiful, living piece of art.

Bonsai trees offer several profound life lessons that can inspire and guide us:

Patience: Growing a bonsai tree requires years of careful attention and nurturing. This teaches us the value of patience and the importance of taking time to achieve our goals.

Balance: Bonsai trees represent harmony between the tree, soil, water, and environment. This reminds us to seek balance in our lives, whether it's between work and personal life, mental and physical well-being, or ambition and contentment.

Resilience: Despite their delicate appearance, bonsai trees can withstand various environmental challenges. They teach us to adapt and persevere through life's difficulties, emerging stronger and more resilient.

Attention to Detail: The meticulous care required for bonsai cultivation highlights the importance of precision and focus. This lesson can be applied to all areas of life, encouraging us to strive for excellence in everything we do.

Appreciation of the Journey: Bonsai trees are living, growing works of art that evolve over time. They remind us to enjoy the journey of life, appreciating the small, beautiful moments along the way.

These lessons from bonsai trees can help us cultivate a more mindful, balanced, and resilient approach to life.

The three human bombs

Bakudan San'yushi - Self-Sacrifice and Death Worship in Imperial Japanese Propaganda

Although historians have claimed that Japanese wartime propaganda was ineffective compared to its American and German counterparts, it still had a profound impact in instilling confidence among the Japanese people. One of the most famous examples of Japanese propaganda is the legend of the Bakudan San'yushi (Nikudan San'yushi), or the Three Human Bombs.

The story became a cultural sensation featured in countless newspapers, radio broadcasts, movies, and even school lessons. Not only did the Three Human Bombs motivate civilians to support the nation's war effort, but it also cemented nationalistic and patriotic values of self-sacrifice and death worship into the whole of Japanese society.

The story is set during the Shanghai Incident (January 28 Incident), five years before the Second Sino-Japanese War. Following the Japanese invasion and occupation of Manchuria, anti-Japanese movements quickly grew throughout China.

The Chinese boycotted Japanese products and led anti-Japanese protests. Leaders of the Japanese Army even encouraged anti-Japanese demonstrations in Shanghai in order to distract Western attention from Manchuria.

The most famous instance of this occurred when the Japanese government sent a group of ultranationalist Japanese Buddhist priests to Shanghai. They provoked the Chinese by shouting anti-Chinese expressions and slogans openly on the streets. Two of these Japanese provocateurs were killed by Chinese workers, leading the Japanese Navy to send forces to protect other Japanese in the city. The Navy faced fierce resistance from the Chinese military and requested army reinforcement. The conflict quickly escalated to a full-out battle.

According to the legend, during the Battle in Shanghai, three army combat engineers from Kyushu—Eshita Takeji, Kitagawa Susumu, and Sakue Inosuke—performed a suicide charge against an enemy stronghold, leading the Japanese Army to overrun the defending Chinese forces. The three soldiers were hailed as heroes and publicly endorsed by Araki Sadao, the Minister of War and Education.

Photograph of the Three Human Bombs from the Osaka Asahi: Eshita Takeji, (left), Sakue Inosuke (center), and Kitagawa Susumu (right)

Imperial Japanese soldiers sacrificing themselves in war and launching suicide attacks is a familiar trope today. Although many associate these acts with samurai values and Japanese culture, suicide attacks were not common in the military until the later years of WWII. The legend of the Three Human Bombs and other Japanese propaganda inspired a new generation of devoted nationalists.

The story became prominent in government-run education programs. School lessons and textbooks altered and exaggerated the legend to fit the patriotic narrative. The following is an excerpt from a government-approved textbook retelling the story:

With Kitagawa Jō [Susumu] in front, Eshita Takeji in the middle, and Sakue Inosuke in the back, the three dash toward the enemy's stronghold carrying a lit Bangalore torpedo. Kitagawa falls to the ground. The other two sappers stumble but stay on their feet. Not one of them let go of the Bangalore torpedo (a metal tube containing explosives).

All the while the fuse continues to burn. Kitagawa is pushed to his feet by courage. Eshita and Sakue move forward to help their comrade recover. Something changes inside them. The three sappers now function as one with the Bangalore torpedo.

As the fuse is just about to reach its end, the three sappers transcend our normal state of existence to become flesh bomb heroes. The Bangalore torpedo pierces the barbed wire. Heaven and earth rumble from the explosion.

Our infantry troops charge forward. The sappers' commanding officer finds Sakue lying on the ground and says 'Sakue, you did well. Do you have any last words?' Sakue replies, 'No, sir. Was the mission a success?' Sakue's broken body is repositioned so that he may view the damaged stronghold for himself. In a loud voice, the commanding officer declares, 'Over there, our brigade is charging through the hole you made.' Sakue responds with a final 'Long Live the Emperor' and then closes his eyes forever.

Furthermore, the story of the Three Human Bombs was heavily featured in mass media. Prominent newspapers such as the Osaka Mainichi and the Asahi Shimbun were quick to feature it.

Asahi even launched a campaign to collect condolence money for the soldiers' families and to fund the creation of a bronze statue of the soldiers in Tokyo. Many artists and creators also adapted the tale into various works, including movies, books, and songs. Six different directors and production companies released films about the Three Human Bombs only a month following the incident.

The story also became popular among children, who were exposed to the Three Human Bombs through manga, children's books, and kamishibai (paper theatre). Many of these children reenacted the story as pretend play. In some cases, it even motivated young adults to commit suicide as acts of self-sacrifice.

For instance, a nineteen-year-old girl in Gifu prefecture drowned herself in a lake. The note she left was addressed to her two brothers who had gone to war and read, 'With tears of admiration, I am following the path of the

Three Human Bombs and I beseech you to do likewise by expending yourselves to the utmost in service to the nation.'

The legend became a successful government and military campaign to indoctrinate the young. The impact of the Three Human Bombs is most evident during the later years of the Pacific War.

Children who learned about the story during the 1930s were now soldiers participating in Japan's last-ditch effort against the Allies, including the Japanese Special Attack Units (tokkōtai or Kamikaze). Concepts of death worship had become normalized and internalized among the Japanese. It became an expectation for Japanese soldiers to die in battle and a disgrace for them to return alive.

Although nearly 80 years have passed since Japan's surrender, we still see the persisting effects of the messages broadcasted by Imperial Japanese propaganda in contemporary Japanese society, as self-sacrifice continues to be an integral part of modern Japanese culture

THE GIRL WITH RED SHOES...

'San Diego' and 'Yokohama,' sister cities located on opposite sides of the Pacific Ocean, share another link—a statue of THE GIRL WITH RED SHOES.

The statue was inspired by the famous Japanese nursery rhyme, 赤い靴 "Red Shoes" written in 1922 by Japanese poet Ujō Noguchi, and then composed into song by Nagayo Motoori.

The poem and song lyrics place the mother on the Yokohama pier, hiding to watch as her little girl—clad in red shoes—leaves to board a ship with blue-eyed foreigners. In the song, the mother cries out how she will think of her daughter every time she sees red shoes and she wonders if one day her daughter will look back across the sea and yearn for home.

While it is widely known in Japan that the beloved nursery rhyme and statues were inspired by the real-life story of Iwasaki Kimi—a young orphan girl from Fushimi, who was given up for adoption due to hardships—the story behind that story isn't as well-known. You see, both the poem and the song took creative liberties in the retelling.

Kimi was born in a small village at the foothills of the old Shizuoka prefecture. The unmarried mother, finding life difficult with an illegitimate child, moved, and when the opportunity presented itself, she married.

To ensure a better life for the child, the woman's new father-in-law arranged for mercenaries to adopt then three-year-old girl and take her to America.

However, the child contracted tuberculosis—then incurable—before setting sail, and was turned over to a nearby orphanage instead, where she remained until she died at the age of nine.

The child's mother and husband never knew.

The city of Yokohama gifted the GIRL WITH RED SHOES statue to stand on the tip of Shelter Island, near the US naval base in San Diego. She stands at each port on either side of the ocean to remind us of the thousands of innocent children lost between them.

The Yellow pumpkin

Japanese artist Yayoi Kusama's iconic, polka-dotted yellow pumpkin sculpture on the island of Naoshima was dislodged Monday due to strong winds and high tide from a typhoon, and has been removed for restoration, the art exhibit confirmed.

Typhoon Lupit made landfall Sunday night in Southwestern Japan, where Naoshima is located, bringing heavy rain and stormy winds throughout Monday.

Videos surfaced on social media of Kusama's "Pumpkin" swept away from the pier, flipped over, and tumbling on the shore as waves tossed it around.

Benesse Art Site, the exhibit that houses "Pumpkin," confirmed on Monday afternoon in a tweet that the sculpture was damaged by the typhoon and was removed so that it can be restored. The exhibit said it would make an announcement once the artwork is on display again.

The "Pumpkin" located on the tip of the pier in Naoshima remains one of the most recognized images of the island, with its vibrant yellow and black polka dots juxtaposed with the bright blue water in the background.

Since it was installed in 1994, the "Pumpkin" has become an iconic staple of the Benesse Art Site of Naoshima, also known as Japan's art island, known for its modern art museums and architecture, and displays of modern sculpture and installations around the island. The sculpture is about two metres tall and just under 2.5 metres wide. It was one of the largest pumpkins that Kusama, known for her colorful shapes and patterns, had made at the time, and was her first open-air sculpture, according to the Benesse Art Site Naoshima.

Kusama then went on to create open-air sculptures, mainly pumpkins, in cities throughout the world. Pumpkins are a source of "radiant energy" and "inspiration for the artist since her childhood, when she was surrounded by her family's seed nursery in prewar Japan," according to the Smithsonian.

The yellow pumpkins were prominently featured in Kusama's 2017 "Infinity Mirrors" exhibition at the Hirshhorn Museum in Washington, and a version of the "Pumpkin" was on display outside of the museum throughout the course of the exhibition.

The "Pumpkin" has been temporarily relocated in advance of a typhoon to preserve it from potential damage. An Instagram video posted in 2019 by the account of Guesthouse Umikko, located near the art display, showed workers manually lifting the pumpkin and transporting it on the back of a truck before a typhoon

The story of Hachiko

Hachiko was born in November 1923 in the city of Odate in Akita prefecture, the original home of Akitas.

A large-sized Japanese dog, the Akita is one of the country's oldest and most popular breeds. Designated by the Japanese government as a national icon in 1931, they were once trained to hunt animals like wild boar and elk.

"Akita dogs are calm, sincere, intelligent, and brave [and] obedient to their masters," said Eietsu Sakuraba, author of an English language children's book about Hachiko. "On the other hand, it also has a stubborn personality and is wary of anyone other than its master."

The year Hachiko was born, Hidesaburo Ueno, a renowned agricultural professor and a dog lover, asked a student to find him an Akita puppy.

After a grueling train journey, the puppy arrived at the Ueno residence in Shibuya district on 15 January 1924, where it was initially thought dead. According to Hachiko's biographer, Prof Mayumi Itoh, Ueno, and his wife Yae nursed him back to health over the next six months.

Ueno named him Hachi, or eight in Japanese. Ko is an honorific bestowed by Ueno's students.

The long wait

Ueno took a train to work several times a week. He was accompanied to Shibuya station by his three dogs, including Hachiko. The trio would then wait there for his return in the evening.

On 21 May 1925, Ueno, then 53, died of a cerebral hemorrhage. Hachiko had been with him for just 16 months.

"While people were attending the wake, Hachi smelled Dr Ueno from the house and went inside the living room. He crawled under the coffin and refused to move," writes Prof Itoh.

Hachiko spent the next few months with different families outside Shibuya but eventually, in the summer of 1925, he ended up with Ueno's gardener Kikusaburo Kobayashi.

Having returned to the area where his late master lived, Hachiko soon resumed his daily commute to the station, rain, or shine.

"In the evening, Hachi stood on four legs at the ticket gate and looked at each passenger as if he were looking for someone," writes Prof Itoh. Station employees initially saw him as a nuisance. Yakitori vendors would pour water on him, and little boys bullied and hit him.

However, he gained nationwide fame after Japanese daily Tokyo Asahi Shimbun wrote about him in October 1932.

The station received donations of food for Hachiko each day, while visitors came from far and wide to see him. Poems and haikus were written about him. A fundraising event in 1934 to make a statue of him reportedly drew a crowd of 3,000.

Hachiko's eventual death on 8 March 1935 made the front page of many newspapers. At his funeral, Buddhist monks offered prayers for him, and dignitaries read eulogies. Thousands visited his statue in the following days.

In impoverished post-war Japan, a fundraising drive for a new statue of Hachiko even managed to raise 800,000 yen, an enormous sum at the time, worth about 4bn yen (£22m; $28m) today.

"In retrospect, I feel that he knew that Dr Ueno would not come back, but he kept waiting - Hachiko taught us the value of keeping faith in someone," wrote Takeshi Okamoto in a newspaper article in 1982. As a high school student, he had seen Hachiko at the station daily.

Remembering Hachiko

Every year on 8 April, a memorial service for Hachiko is held outside Shibuya Station. His statue is often decorated with scarves, Santa hats and, most recently, a surgical mask.

His mount is on display at the National Museum of Nature and Science in Tokyo. Some of his remains are interred at the Aoyama Cemetery, alongside Ueno and Yae. Statues of him have also been cast in Odate, Ueno's hometown Hisai, the University of Tokyo and Rhode Island, the American setting for the 2009 movie.

Will the world's most loyal dog still be celebrated a century from now? Prof Yano says yes because she believes the "heroism of Hachiko" is not defined by any particular period - rather it is timeless.

Mr. Sakuraba is equally optimistic. "Even 100 years from now, this unconditional, devoted love will remain unchanged, and the story of Hachiko will live on forever".

CHAPTER 10

RELIGIONS OF JAPAN

Religious tolerance is practiced in Japan. Can you believe that Japan has more than 500 religions. You can not hear religious fights in Japan. Majority of these 500 religious cults have few followers and except the major religions like Shintoism, Buddhism, etc.

Let us look at some interesting aspects of the major religions and their adherents.

The total number of adherents outnumber the entire population. Isn't amazing.

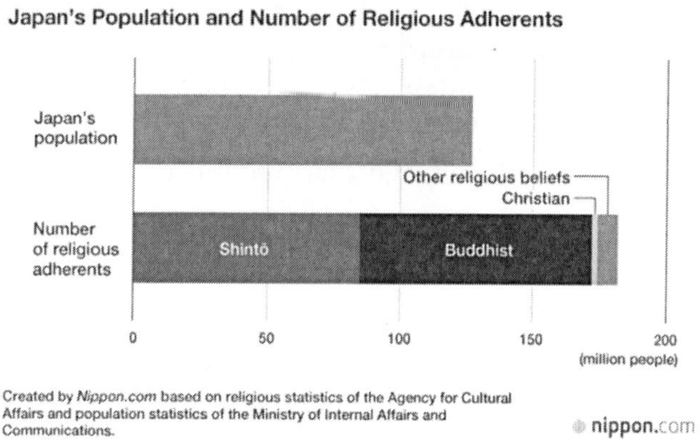

One reason the number of adherents exceeds the population is that, due to the freedom of religious belief in Japan and the separation of church and state, there is minimal government intervention in religious affairs. Religious groups provide statistics on a voluntary basis and are free to define "adherent" however they wish. In some past surveys, the overall number of adherents has even exceeded 200 million.

The Japanese view of religion also plays a part. In Japan, there was an intermingling between the Indigenous Shinto faith and the Buddhism that was introduced from the Asian continent around the sixth century. The amalgamation of those two beliefs lasted for over a thousand years until the Meiji government ordered the separation of the two faiths in the late nineteenth century. There was no real awareness of being an adherent, since neither tradition had a conversion ceremony, but the practices of both took root in people's lives in the form of daily rituals and seasonal events.

The fascinating origins, history, and evolution of Shintoism, Buddhism, and Zen Buddhism:

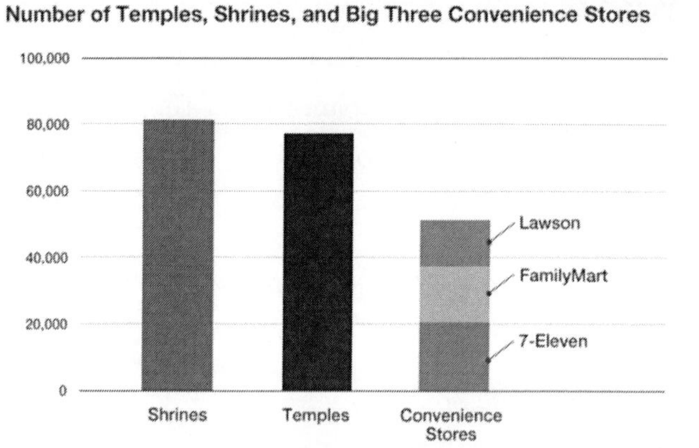

Created by *Nippon.com* based on religious statistics of the Agency for Cultural Affairs and data disclosed by each of the convenience store companies; store numbers for 7-Eleven and FamilyMart are as of May 31, 2018, and for Lawson as of February 28, 2018.

	Temples	Shrines
1	Aichi Prefecture 4,589	Niigata Prefecture 4,732
2	Osaka Prefecture 3,389	Hyōgo Prefecture 3,864
3	Hyōgo Prefecture 3,289	Fukuoka Prefecture 3,421
4	Shiga Prefecture 3,213	Aichi Prefecture 3,359
5	Kyoto Prefecture 3,077	Gifu Prefecture 3,272

Shintoism

There are approximately 80000 Shinto shrines in Japan. Shintoism and Hinduism have lots of similarities.

Origin: Shinto, meaning "way of the gods," is Japan's oldest religion. It evolved from ancient animistic beliefs and practices prevalent in Japan. During the Yayoi culture period (around 300 BCE to 300 CE), the foundations of Shinto were laid.

Key Concepts: Purity, harmony, family respect, and subordination of the individual before the group.

Beliefs and Practices:

Kami: Gods, spirits, and supernatural forces inhabit natural places of beauty.

No Founder: Unlike many religions, Shinto has no recognized founder.

Mythical Origins: The Kojiki and Nihon Shoki describe the "Age of the Gods" and the lineage from the seven Buddhas to Bodhidharma, who introduced Buddhism to China.

Inseparable from Japanese Culture: Shinto has become intertwined with Japanese life, whether or not individuals claim religious affiliation.

Top 5 Shinto shrines in Japan

1. Fushimi Inari Shrine – Southern Kyoto
2. Ise Grand Shrine – Ise city
3. Itsukushima Shrine – Miyajima Island, Hiroshima
4. Toshogu Shrine – Nikko

5. Izumo Taisha – Izumo city

Buddhism

There are approximately 80000 Buddhist temples in Japan. (Including three major sects of Zen)

There are eleven major sects of Buddhism at present as follows:

- Hosso – Shu
- Ji – Shu
- Jodo – shu
- Kegon – Shu
- Nichiren – Shu
- Ritsu – Shu
- Shin – Shu
- Tendai – Shu
- Yuzu – Nembutsu – Shu
- Zen – Shu
    - Soto
    - Rinzai
    - Obaku

Founder: Founded by Siddhartha Gautama (the Buddha) over 2,500 years ago in India.

Beliefs and Practices:

Enlightenment: Focus on achieving inner peace and wisdom. Awakening leads to nirvana.

No Supreme God: No deity to worship; Buddha is considered extraordinary but not divine.

Path to Enlightenment: Morality, meditation, and wisdom.

Karma and Reincarnation: Law of cause and effect and the continuous cycle of rebirth.

Spread: Buddhism spread to China, Korea, Vietnam, and Japan.

Overlap with Other Faiths: Many Buddhist ideas overlap with other religions.

Top 7 Buddhist temples in Japan

1. Kiyomizu-dera Temple (Kyoto)
2. Kinkakuji Temple (Kyoto)
3. Senso-ji Temple (Tokyo)
4. Hokokuji Temple (Kamakura)
5. Todai-ji Temple (Nara)
6. Sanjusangendo Temple (Kyoto)
7. Shitennoji Temple (Osaka)

Zen Buddhism

Origins: Zen (Chan in China, Sŏn in Korea, Thien in Vietnam) emerged in China around the 5th century CE. It emphasizes meditation (dhyana) and awakening.

Nature of Zen Teaching:

Awakening for All: Anyone can achieve awakening but needs instruction from a master.

Secular Arts: Associated with tea ceremonies, ink painting, and gardening.

Modern Connotations: Often associated with artistic or spiritual vitality regardless of context.

Genealogical Lineage: Traced from the seven Buddhas to Bodhidharma, who introduced true Buddhism to China in the 5th century.

Zen in Japan: Influential in Japan, especially through secular arts and spontaneous expression.

Top 6 Zen temples in Japan (Kyoto)

1. Nanzen-ji Temple
2. Tenryu-ji Temple
3. Shokokuji Temple
4. Kennin-ji Temple
5. Tofukuji Temple
6. Manju-ji Temple

"Sojiji temple" near Kawasaki is also a very important Zen temple, belongs to Soto Zen Sect. The Zazen meditation classes conducted here are very good. I have attended one session in English, and it was wonderful experience.

Kamakura and Kyoto are two places in Japan which are full of temples and shrines.

In summary, Shintoism is deeply rooted in Japan's ancient animistic beliefs, Buddhism spread across Asia, and Zen emphasizes meditation and awakening. Each has left an indelible mark on cultural and spiritual life.

How to pray in a Shinto Shrine

As soon as you enter the main Torri (An orange colored gate) of the shrine, bow once. then,

Purification: Upon entering the shrine, you'll find a water pavilion called a 'temizuya' for cleansing before you approach the gods. Here are the steps for purification at a Chozuya:

Hold the ladle in your right hand and pour water over your left.

Change hands and pour water over your right hand.

Change hands again and pour water over your left hand and then using this water take it into your mouth (then spit delicately into the drain; not the basin).

Lastly, take the water into the ladle once more and raising the scoop into the air letting the water run down the hand – this cleans the object for the next worshipper.

Approach the Haiden: The 'haiden' is where you pay your respects to the kami-sama. Approach the offertory box called a 'saisen-bako,' but avoid standing dead-center in front of it. This space is known as the 'sei-chuu,' the passageway that the gods walk through.

Make an Offering: Gently drop or toss an offering into the saisen-bako. While it's less about the amount of the offering than the sincerity of your prayers, superstition dictates that certain yen amounts bring good or bad luck. The five-yen coin is considered a good choice because it sounds like 'go-en', the Japanese word for luck.

Pray: After making an offering, ring the bell to signal your presence to the local deity. Then, bow twice, clap your hands twice, pray while keeping your hands together, and finally bow once again.

Please note that some shrines may have their own individual style of prayer. It's always a good idea to observe others or ask for guidance if you're unsure.

How to pray at the Buddhist temple

Preparation: Before praying, take a deep breath, get comfortable, and close your eyes. You may want to light candles or incense to help calm yourself down and bring yourself closer to your prayer.

Mantras: Mantras are phrases meant to be repeated over and over again1. They help you avoid distraction and focus on your prayers. Some common mantras include "Om mani padme hum," "Oṃ Amideva Hrīḥ," and "Om A Ra Pa Ca Na Dhih".

My favorite has always been the "Heart Sutra."

Prayer for the Three Jewels: This is a short prayer that can be repeated as a mantra1. It goes as follows:

I take refuge in the Buddha, Dharma, and Sangha

Until I attain Enlightenment.

By merit accumulations from practicing generosity and the other perfections

May I attain Enlightenment, for the benefit of all sentient beings.

Pray for the happiness and wellbeing of your friends and family: This prayer helps you stay thankful for the people around you, and to recognize their connection1. It goes as follows:

May I be well, happy, and peaceful.
May my teachers be well, happy, and peaceful.
May my parents be well, happy, and peaceful.
May my relatives be happy

How to pray at a Zen temple

Preparation: Before praying, take a deep breath, get comfortable, and close your eyes1. You may want to light candles or incense to help calm yourself down and bring yourself closer to your prayer.

Mantras: Mantras are phrases meant to be repeated over and over again1. They help you avoid distraction and focus on your prayers1. Some common mantras include "Om mani padme hum," "Oṃ Amideva Hrīḥ," and "Om A Ra Pa Ca Na Dhih".

Prayer for the Three Jewels: This is a short prayer that can be repeated as a mantra1. It goes as follows:

I take refuge in the Buddha, Dharma, and Sangha

Until I attain Enlightenment.

By merit accumulations from practicing generosity and the other perfections

May I attain Enlightenment, for the benefit of all sentient beings.

Pray for the happiness and wellbeing of your friends and family: This prayer helps you stay thankful for the people around you, and to recognize their connection1. It goes as follows:

May I be well, happy, and peaceful.
May my teachers be well, happy, and peaceful.
May my parents be well, happy, and peaceful.
May my relatives be well, happy, and peaceful.
May my friends be well, happy, and peaceful.

Approach the Main Hall: In front of the main hall, quietly put a donation into the offertory box and say a prayer. The thing to remember here is to not clap your hands like you would when praying at a Shinto shrine! At a temple, the correct way to pray is by silently putting your hands together.

Bow: Simply bow at a slight angle (some suggest 45 degrees is ideal), put your hands together, and offer up your prayers. Bow once more before leaving the main hall, and also as you exit the temple precincts.

If you are in doubt, just follow what the locals do.

Hindu deities and their representations in Japanese culture:

Hindu gods in Japanese culture

The religious landscape of Japan is a fascinating blend of Shintoism, Buddhism, and other traditions. Across cultures, India and Japan share ancient connections through their gods. Many Hindu deities are actively worshipped in Japan, with hundreds of shrines dedicated to them. Deities such as Lakshmi, Shiva, and Ganesh are also present in the representations of Japanese culture. Incorporating Hindu gods into Japanese culture, they are worshipped alongside Japanese deities in a combination of Shintoism and Buddhism. The manifestation of this demonstrates a significant cultural exchange and the preservation of traditional practices.

Lord Ganesha and Kangiten

Kangiten, like Ganesha, is an elephant-headed god in Japanese mythology. Kangiten is often depicted as a male-female pair in an embrace. He is worshipped as the god of bliss and remover of difficulties, bestowing success, health, and prosperity upon his devotees, mirroring the role of Ganesha in Hinduism. This syncretism highlights the shared reverence for deities who can overcome obstacles and bring good fortune.

Maa Saraswati and Benzaiten

Benzaiten, derived from the Hindu goddess Saraswati, is revered as one of the Seven Lucky Gods (Shichi Fukujin) in Japan. Both goddesses are associated with eloquence, intellect, speech, knowledge, and music. In an article with TOI, Devdutt Pattanaik noted that Benzaiten is not only worshipped for knowledge and music but also for wealth, prosperity, fertility, and beauty, similar to Lakshmi. She is also visualised with multiple arms holding swords, like Durga, and was worshipped by the Samurai as a warrior.

Lord Shiva and Daikoku

Daikoku, another lord of the Shichi Fukujin, shares connections with the Hindu god Shiva. Both are considered gods of darkness. Daikoku is sometimes manifested as a female deity, Daikokunyo or Daikokutennyo, a form of Mahakala in Hindu mythology. Daikoku is often depicted holding a golden mallet and standing on bales of rice, symbolising wealth and prosperity. This representation reflects his role as a god of fortune and abundance in Japanese culture.

Goddess Lakshmi and Kichijoten

Kichijoten, sometimes included among the Shichi Fukujin, is derived from the Hindu goddess Lakshmi. Both goddesses are worshipped as providers of fertility, beauty, wealth and happiness. Kichijoten is often depicted as a beautiful woman, embodying the qualities of grace and abundance. This reflects the shared reverence for goddesses who bring prosperity and well-being.

Indra Dev and Taishakuten

Taishakuten, derived from the Hindu god Indra, shares many similarities with his Indian counterpart. Both are often depicted riding an elephant, a symbol of power and majesty. Taishakuten is a prominent deity in Japan, with numerous temples dedicated to him. He is revered as a god of protection and is often associated with warriors.

Vaisravana/Kubera and Bishamonten

Bishamonten, also one of the Shichi Fukujin, is derived from the Hindu god Kubera, also known as Vaisravana. They are worshipped as gods of warriors and protectors, dispensing fortune and punishing wrongdoers. Bishamonten is often depicted holding a pagoda or spear and riding a lion, symbolising his strength and guardianship. This reflects his role as a defender of the Buddhist faith and a protector of the country.

Yama and Enma

In Japanese mythology, Enma mirrors Yama from Hindu tradition, both presiding over the realm of the dead. Enma, like Yama, is believed to be the head of hell, responsible for judging the crimes of the deceased. He is often depicted as an expression of fury, a stern judge who ensures justice in the afterlife. This parallel highlights the shared concepts of justice and retribution in both Hindu and Japanese beliefs, where Yama and Enma hold similar roles in the cosmic order.

CHAPTER 11

JAPAN'S ECONOMY

Japan's economy is diverse, with several key industries contributing significantly to its GDP. Here are the major industries and their contributions:

Services: The largest sector, contributing approximately 71.39% to Japan's GDP in 2022. This includes finance, retail, real estate, and various professional services.

Industry: Accounts for about 26.92% of the GDP. This sector includes manufacturing, construction, and mining. Key industries within this sector are:

Automotive: Japan is a global leader in automobile manufacturing, with companies like Toyota, Honda, and Nissan.

Electronics: Renowned for consumer electronics, semiconductors, and robotics, with major players like Sony, Panasonic, and Toshiba.

Machinery: Includes industrial machinery and equipment, contributing significantly to exports.

Agriculture: Although a smaller sector, it still plays a role, contributing around 1.02% to the GDP. Japan produces rice, vegetables, and fruits, and is known for its high-quality agricultural products.

These industries collectively drive Japan's economic growth and maintain its position as one of the world's largest economies.

Centuries old companies in Japan

It is interesting to note that Japan has many Centuries old companies, still exist.

The oldest company in Japan is Kongō Gumi, a construction company founded in 578 AD. This makes it not only the oldest company in Japan but also the oldest continuously operating company in the world. Kongō Gumi specializes in the design, construction, restoration, and repair of shrines, temples, castles, and other cultural heritage buildings.

Isn't it fascinating how a company can sustain itself for over 1,450 years?

Here are some other ancient companies that have stood the test of time:

1. Nishiyama Onsen Keiunkan (Japan) - Founded in 705 AD, this hot spring hotel has been operated by the same family for over 1,300 years.

2. Koman (Japan) - Established in 717 AD, this ryokan (traditional Japanese inn) has been welcoming guests for centuries.
3. Hōshi Ryokan (Japan) - Founded in 718 AD, another historic ryokan that has been in operation for over 1,300 years.
4. Genda Shigyō (Japan) - Established in 771 AD, this company specializes in ceremonial paper goods.
5. Tanaka-Iga (Japan) - Established in 885 AD, this company produces religious goods.

It's amazing how these companies have managed to preserve their heritage and continue their operations through centuries of change.

The software market in Japan is experiencing significant growth and transformation. Here are some key points:

Market Size and Growth: The Japanese software market generated a revenue of approximately USD 23.7 billion in 2024 and is projected to reach around USD 50 billion by 2030, growing at a compound annual growth rate (CAGR) of 13.1% from 2025 to 2030 .

Key Segments: The market includes various segments such as application software, system infrastructure software, and development and deployment software. Application software is the largest and fastest-growing segment.

Technological Trends: The market is heavily influenced by advancements in cloud computing, cybersecurity, and artificial intelligence (AI). The adoption of cloud services is helping companies reduce costs and increase flexibility.

Digital Transformation: Ongoing digital transformation initiatives are reshaping how businesses operate and communicate, driving demand for innovative software solutions .

Overall, the software market in Japan is poised for robust growth, driven by technological advancements and increasing digitalization across various industries.

Japan hosts several leading software companies that have made significant contributions to the global tech industry. Here are some of the top players:

Leading Software companies in Japan

ITOCHU Techno-Solutions: A major provider of software and technical consulting services.

NTT Data Group: Known for its extensive IT services and solutions.

Fujitsu: Offers a wide range of software and IT consulting services.

NEC Corporation: Specializes in IT and network solutions.

SYLA Technologies: Focuses on business intelligence and software development.

OBIC Co., Ltd.: A prominent player in the software application industry.

Oracle Corporation Japan: Provides enterprise software solutions .

DeNA Co., Ltd.: Known for its mobile and online services.

SHIFT, Inc.: Specializes in software testing and quality assurance.

Sansan, Inc.: Offers cloud-based contact management solutions.

These companies are driving innovation and growth in Japan's software market, contributing to various sectors such as IT services, business intelligence, and enterprise solutions.

Leading Technology companies of Japan

Japan is home to numerous influential technology companies that have made significant contributions to various sectors. Here are a few notable ones:

Sony Group Corporation: Renowned globally for its consumer electronics, entertainment, and gaming products.

Fujitsu: A major player in IT services and solutions, providing a wide range of technology products.

Canon Inc.: Famous for its imaging and optical products, including cameras and printers.

NEC: Specializes in IT and network solutions, contributing to advancements in telecommunications.

Renesas Electronics: A leading provider of semiconductor solutions.

Keyence: Known for its innovative automation and scientific instruments.

Panasonic Corp: Offers a diverse range of consumer electronics and home appliances.

Tokyo Electron Ltd: A key player in semiconductor manufacturing equipment.

Trend Micro: Provides cybersecurity solutions to protect against digital threats.

Murata Manufacturing Co. Ltd: Specializes in electronic components and solutions.

These companies are just a few examples of Japan's robust technology sector, which continues to drive innovation and influence global markets.

Leading Automobile companies in Japan

Japan is renowned for its automobile industry, which includes several globally recognized companies. Here are some of the key players:

Toyota Motor Corporation: The largest automobile manufacturer in Japan, known for its reliable and innovative vehicles.

Honda Motor Co., Ltd.: Famous for its cars, motorcycles, and power equipment.

Nissan Motor Co., Ltd.: A major player in electric vehicles and known for its diverse range of cars.

Suzuki Motor Corporation: Specializes in compact cars and motorcycles.

Mazda Motor Corporation: Known for its stylish designs and innovative engineering.

Subaru Corporation: Renowned for its all-wheel-drive vehicles and boxer engines.

Mitsubishi Motors Corporation: Offers a wide range of vehicles, including electric and hybrid models.

Isuzu Motors Ltd.: Focuses on commercial vehicles and diesel engines.

Daihatsu Motor Co., Ltd.: Specializes in small cars and kei cars.

Lexus: Toyota's luxury vehicle division, known for its high-end cars.

These companies have significantly contributed to the global automotive industry with their innovative technologies and diverse vehicle offerings.

Recently,(in the year 2025) Honda, Nissan, and Mitsubishi Motors have agreed to merge, creating a significant shift in Japan's auto industry.

This merger aims to bolster their position against rising competition from electric vehicle manufacturers, particularly from China.

The combined entity is set to become the world's third-largest automaker by sales.

CHAPTER 12

INDO JAPAN RELATIONSHIP

India-Japan Trade Links:

India and Japan share a robust and dynamic trade relationship, rooted in historical ties and mutual economic interests. This partnership has evolved significantly over the years, marked by substantial growth in bilateral trade and collaborative ventures in various sectors.

Historical Context

The diplomatic relations between India and Japan were formally established in 1952. However, the cultural and spiritual connections date back centuries, with notable interactions such as the visit of Indian monk Bodhisena to Japan in 752 AD. These deep-rooted ties have laid a strong foundation for the modern economic partnership.

Trade Statistics

In the fiscal year 2023-24, the bilateral trade between India and Japan totaled US$ 22.85 billion . Japan's exports to India amounted to US$ 17.69 billion, while India's exports to Japan were US$ 5.15 billion. This trade volume highlights the significant economic interdependence between the two nations.

Major Exports and Imports

Japan's primary exports to India include nuclear reactors, copper, electrical machinery, and organic chemicals. Specifically, Japan exported US$ 3.33 billion worth of nuclear reactors and US$ 2.24 billion worth of copper to India in FY24 .

On the other hand, India's major exports to Japan comprise engineering goods, organic and inorganic chemicals, marine products, and gems and jewelry. For instance, India exported US$ 1.92 billion worth of engineering goods and US$ 881.45 million worth of organic and inorganic chemicals to Japan during the same period.

Recent Trends and Developments

The trade relationship between India and Japan has seen consistent growth. In March 2025, Japan's exports to India increased by 14.4% from the previous year, reaching ¥277 billion . This growth reflects the strengthening economic ties and the increasing demand for Japanese products in India.

Moreover, the two countries have embarked on collaborative projects, such as the co-development of the Unified Complex Radio Antenna (UNICORN) mast for Indian Navy ships . This initiative marks the first co-development of defense equipment between India and Japan, highlighting the depth of their strategic partnership.

Economic Impact

The trade links between India and Japan have a profound impact on both economies. Japan ranks 17th in India's total trade, accounting for 2.1% of India's trade volume . Conversely, India ranks 18th in Japan's total trade, with a 1.4% share . These figures underscore the importance of bilateral trade in the economic landscapes of both nations.

India and Japan's trade relationship is characterized by mutual benefits and strategic collaborations. The continuous growth in trade volume and the diversification of traded goods highlight the dynamic nature of this partnership. As both countries continue to explore new avenues for cooperation, the future of India-Japan trade links looks promising and poised for further expansion.

Japan has established several manufacturing facilities across India, contributing significantly to the industrial landscape. Here are some notable examples:

1. Maruti Suzuki India Ltd.
   - Locations: Gurugram and Manesar in Haryana, with an R&D center in Rohtak, Haryana.
   - Sector: Automotive manufacturing.
   - Details: Maruti Suzuki is a leading passenger vehicle manufacturer in India, with Suzuki Motor Corporation holding a significant equity stake.

2. Toyota Kirloskar Motor Pvt. Ltd.
   - Location: Bidadi, Karnataka.
   - Sector: Automotive manufacturing.
   - Details: Toyota Kirloskar Motor is a joint venture between Toyota Motor Corporation and Kirloskar Group, producing a range of vehicles for the Indian market.

3. Panasonic Life Solutions India Pvt. Ltd.
   - Location: Gurgaon, Haryana
   - Sector: Electronics and electrical solutions.
   - Details: Panasonic manufactures a variety of electronic products and solutions, contributing to the consumer electronics and industrial sectors.

4. Japan Industrial Townships (JITs)
   - Locations: Various states including Gujarat, Tamil Nadu, Rajasthan, Andhra Pradesh, Maharashtra, Karnataka, Haryana, and Uttar Pradesh
   - Sector: Multiple sectors including automotive, electronics, and machinery.

- Details: JITs are special industrial zones developed to attract Japanese investments and facilitate manufacturing activities.

These facilities highlight the diverse industrial presence of Japanese companies in India, spanning automotive, electronics, and other sectors.

Prime Minister of INDIA Shri. Narendra Modi's ambitious project of having bullet train in the country, is maturing into a reality.

Japan plays a crucial role in India's first bullet train project, the Mumbai-Ahmedabad High-Speed Rail (MAHSR). Here are some key contributions and involvement details:

1. Technology and Expertise:
   - Japan is providing its renowned Shinkansen technology for the project. The bullet trains will be based on the Shinkansen E5 series, capable of speeds up to 320 km/h .
   - Japanese expertise in high-speed rail construction and operation is being leveraged to ensure the project's success .

2. Financial Support:
   - The project is primarily funded through low-interest yen loans from Japan, covering approximately 80% of the total project cost.

This financial assistance is crucial for the project's feasibility and implementation.

3. Train Sets and Trials:
   - Japan will supply two Shinkansen train sets for initial inspection and performance testing . These trains will undergo comprehensive trials to assess their performance in India's specific terrain and climate conditions.
   - The first Shinkansen bullet train has already entered the trial phase in Japan, marking a significant milestone for the project.

4. Infrastructure Development:
   - The project involves the construction of a 508-km-long high-speed rail line linking Mumbai and Ahmedabad . This infrastructure is expected to drastically reduce travel time between the two cities from six hours to just two hours .

5. Strategic Partnership:
   - The collaboration between India and Japan on this project is part of a broader strategic partnership aimed at enhancing infrastructure and connectivity in India . This partnership also aligns with the G7's Partnership for Global Infrastructure and Investment (PGII) initiative .

Japan's involvement in the MAHSR project underscores the strong bilateral ties and mutual commitment to advancing infrastructure and technology in India.

DID YOU KNOW

Japanese and Tamil language connection

Professor 'Susumu Ono' of Gakushuin University proposed a provocative hypothesis in 1981, suggesting an ancient link between Japanese and Tamil languages. He asserted that both languages share a common ancestry, supported by similarities in linguistics, sounds, words, grammar, literature, archaeology, and folklore. Ono's research compared the Yayoi burials in Japan with the Megalithic burials of South India and Sri Lanka, revealing remarkable similarities.

CHAPTER 13

JAPANESE LANGUAGE

Japanese writing system

The Japanese writing system uses three main scripts: Hiragana, Katakana, and Kanji. Each has its own unique role and usage:

Hiragana (ひらがな)

- Function: Hiragana is primarily used for native Japanese words and grammatical elements like particles, verb endings, and conjunctions.
- Appearance: It consists of 46 basic characters, each representing a syllable. The characters are curvy and flowing.
- Usage: It's often the first script learned by Japanese children and beginners in Japanese. For example, the word for "cat" (ねこ, neko) is written in hiragana.

Katakana (カタカナ)

- Function: Katakana is used for foreign loanwords, names of foreign places and people, onomatopoeia, and for emphasis (similar to italics in English).

- Appearance: Like hiragana, katakana also has 46 basic characters, but they are more angular and geometric.
- Usage: For instance, the word "television" (テレビ, terebi) is written in katakana.

Kanji (漢字)

- Function: Kanji are logographic characters borrowed from Chinese. Each kanji represents a meaning or concept and can have multiple readings (pronunciations).
- Appearance: Kanji characters are more complex and can range from simple to highly intricate.
- Usage: Kanji are used for most nouns, verbs, adjectives, and proper names. For example, the word for "mountain" (山, yama) is written in kanji.

A literate Japanese person typically knows around 3,500 to 4,000 kanji

Relationships and Usage

- Combination: Japanese text often combines all three scripts. For example, a sentence might use kanji for the main words, hiragana for grammatical elements, and katakana for foreign words.
- Learning Order: Typically, learners start with hiragana, then move on to katakana, and finally tackle kanji due to its complexity.

Understanding how these scripts work together is key to mastering Japanese reading and writing

Note: Japanese script is traditionally written vertically due to historical and practical reasons, although recent times, horizontal writing is gaining momentum.

本 (*hon*) - Book

ベッド (*beddo*) – Bed

誕生日(*tanjōby*) – Birthday

時計 (*tokei*) – Watch, clock

名前 (*namae*) – Name

きれい (*kirei*) – Beautiful

黒い (*kuroi*) – Black

白い (*shiroi*) - White

英語 (*eigo*) – English (language)

大学 (*daigaku*) – University

電話 (*denwa*) – Telephone

バス (*basu*) – Bus

猫 (*neko*) – Cat

犬(*inu*) – Dog

コンピュータ (*konpiūta*) – Computer

服 (*fuku*) – Clothes

Basic Japanese Food Vocabulary

コーヒー (*kohi*) – Coffee

パン (*pan*) – Bread

ビール (*biru*) – Beer

昼ご飯 (*hirogohan*) - Lunch

夕食(*yūshoku*) – Dinner

食べ物 (*tabemono*) – Food

飲み物 (*nomi mono*) – Beverage

果物 (*kudamono*) - Fruit

男の子(*otoko no ko*) – Boy

女の子(*onna no ko*) – Girl

子供 (*kodomo*) – Child

母(*haha*) – Mother

父(*chichi*) – Father

友達 (*tomodachi*) – Friend

学生(*kagusei*) – Student

先生(*sensei*) – Teacher

Basic Japanese Nature Words

川 (*kawa*) – River

花 (*hana*) – Flower

魚(*sakana*) – Fish

空 (*sora*) - Sky

山(*yama*) – Mountain

雨(*ame*) – Rain

今 (*ima*) – Now

今日(*kyou*) – Today

昨日(*kinou*) – Yesterday

明日(*asita*) – Tomorrow

毎日(*mai nichi*) – Every day

毎週 (*maishū*) – Every week

午前 (*gozen*)* - Morning

午後 (*gogo*) – Afternoon

月曜日(*getsuyoubi*) – Monday

火曜日(*kayoubi*) – Tuesday

水曜日(*suiyoubi*) – Wednesday

木曜日(*mokuyoubi*) – Thursday

金曜日(*kinyoubi*) – Friday

土曜日(*douyoubi*) - Saturday

日曜日(*nichiyoubi*) – Sunday

今年 (*k*otosh*i*) – This year

Japanese Body Parts Vocabulary for Beginners

耳(*mimi*) - Ear

手(*te*) - Hand

足(*ashi*) - Foot

目(*me*) - Eye

口(*kuchi*) – Mouth

顔 (*kao*) - Face

Japanese Words for Places and Directions

駅 (*eki*) – Train station

北 (*kita*) – North

南 (*minami*) – South

西(*nishi*) – West

東 (*higashi*) – East

国 (*kuni*) – Country

外国 (*gaikoku*) – Foreign

右 (*mighi*) – Right

左 (*hidari*) – Left

入口(*iriguchi*) – Entrance

出口(*deguchi*) – Exit

Japanese Greetings for Beginners

おはようございます (*ohayou gozaimasu*) – Good Morning

おはよう (*ohayou*) – Good Morning (informal version)

こんにちは (*konnichi wa*) – Hello

こんばんは (*konban wa*) – Good evening

ただいま (*tadaima*) – I'm home (this greeting is used when youget home and want to announce your presence)

おやすみなさい (*oyasuminasai*) Good night (used to announce that you are going to bed. However, you cannot use it when youare leaving someone else's house for the night.)

もしもし (*moshi moshi*) – Hello? (used when answering thephone)

いらっしゃいませ (*irasshiaimase*) – Welcome! (this greeting is mainly used by business owners or employees to welcome their costumers to their store).

おげんきですか (*ogenki desu ka?*) – How Are you?

おしゃしぶりです (*oshashiburi desu*) – Long time no see.

さようなら (*sayounara*) – Goodbye

またね (*matane*) – See you

Common Japanese Phrases for Beginners

はい (*hai*) – Yes

いいえ (*iie*) - No

わかりません (*wakarimasen*) – I don't understand

わすれました (*wasuremashita*) – I forgot

しりません (*shirimasen*) – I don't know

たぶん (*tabun*) – Maybe

だいじょうぶ (*daijoubu*) – Alright

よろしくお願いします (*yoroshiku onegai shimasu*) – Nice to meet you

どうも (*doumo*) – Thanks

おねがいします (*onegai shimasu*) – Please

どうもありがとうございます (*doumo arigatou gozaimasu*) –Thank you so much

すみません (*sumimasen*) – Excuse me / I'm sorry

ごめんなさい (*gomennasai*) – I'm sorry

どういたしまして (*douita shimashite*) – You're welcome

どうぞ* (*douzo*) – After you

助けてください (*tasukete kudasai*) – Help!

Some of the great Indian personalities who visited Japan

Rabindranath Tagore

Tagore visited Japan multiple times, with his first visit in 1916. He was deeply impressed by Japanese art and culture, particularly their intimacy with nature. He admired the Japanese for their artistic sensibilities and simplicity .

However, he also expressed concern over Japan's growing nationalism and warned against imitating Western imperialism. He appreciated the Japanese for their ability to blend art with cleanliness and their deep connection with nature .

I had the privilege to visit Sankeien Garden, where Rabindranath Tagore was staying for few weeks, and they still maintain it as a memorial building.

Netaji Subhas Chandra Bose

Netaji Subhas Chandra Bose sought Japan's assistance during World War II to fight against British colonial rule in India.

He admired Japan's military strength and strategic capabilities. Bose believed that Japan's support was crucial for India's independence movement

He also appreciated the Japanese for their discipline and dedication

Swami Vivekananda

Swami Vivekananda visited Japan in 1893 on his way to the Parliament of Religions in Chicago. He was fascinated by the Japanese people's patriotism, cleanliness, and artistic skills. Vivekananda admired their dedication to their country and their ability to combine art with absolute cleanliness

He encouraged young Indians to visit Japan to learn from their discipline and national pride.

Mata Ne…